BIRDS
and
CAGES

Birds and CAGES

Ida Tomshinsky

Copyright © 2019 by Ida Tomshinsky.

ISBN: Hardcover   978-1-7960-2211-7
          Softcover   978-1-7960-2210-0
          eBook   978-1-7960-2209-4

Print information available on the last page.

Rev. date: 03/15/2019

CONTENTS

Fascinated by Gulls 1

Foreword..3

Common Birds: Doves and Pigeons................................ 11

Ancient Enclosures.. 19

Pet Birds Developments 23

Bird-Catching and Bird-Watching Traditions.............. 37

Step Forward for Pet Birds 51

Metaphoric Symbolism..59

Repurposing Bird Cages in Modern Times 73

Guide to the Masterpieces in Literature, TV, and Movies,

Where Birds are Taking the Central Part, Literary or Symbolic 85

References.. 93

Fascinated by Gulls

The seagulls fascinate me
As they fly from ocean to sea,
Very high
In the sky.

The gulls bring me a smile and a delight,
And some within depth of any storm fight.
The gentle strangers
Are the Earth's angels.

When I was a young girl,
I wished I could sour
From the seashore
Through the air with seagull and whirl.

It is fun to watch the graceful birds,
As they sail over the blue waters.
It stirs my devotion
By captured emotion.

The carefree birds call
Is anything but boring at all,
And for this, "Thank you, gulls! –
I got you a plastic bag with bread crumbs."

I learned from life what we should give and make,
Not what we can take.
Every day brings me light from darkness
And inner grace of the rightness.
(Tomshinsky, 2007)

FOREWORD

Men have held a fascination with birds for a very long time. To us, humans, bird watching activity comes naturally. In general, we are a nation of wildlife lovers; and everyone has an extra love feeling for birds. What is so special and unique about birds? For different people, there are different answers. For some, watching birds in a natural habitat is an effective and reliable way to gain a perspective and to relieve stress. To others, they are so magical. They are interesting to watch because they are beautiful, because birds are inspiring, and fascinating. For example, brown pelicans are the coolest birds. They show off – fly fast aerodynamically a few inches off the water, touch down then drift, as if nothing happened. Or they dive like shooting stars, but on impact they bounce, and fly off with beak full of the catch of the moment.

Birds are cheery and lovable. Birds make life beautiful. Their songs wake us up and put us in a great mood. For me, birds' songs are made of the most beautiful sounds in the nature. Not everyone knows, only male birds are singing. The complex pitch, rhythm, and structure of true birdsongs must be learned in early life. For instant, to attract the mate, a male bird calls other birds from the forest. Some birds like parrots or superb lyrebird know how to imitate human voice or any other sounds. Captive birds have been recorded not only the owners' talk, but also the ability to mimic the industrial sounds of surrounding such as chain saws, car alarms, and even, the camera shutters.

One hundred years ago, the staggering destruction of birdlife caused by the plume trade spurred the passage of the *Migratory Bird Treaty Act*, one of the earliest environmental laws passed anywhere in the world. While fashion trends of putting a dead bird on a hat have changed, the law remains strong, and it is more important as ever to protect birds to live their nature-free lives in modern times. Birds now face the 21st-century threats – naming just some – gas flares, oil spills, oil waste pits, transmission lines, wind and power turbines and more. The act has been used to help reduce those impacts and to implement practices that save birds' lives. The *National Geographic* magazine, National Audubon Society, the Cornel Lab of Ornithology, and BirdLife International joined together forces and resources with more than hundred other organization and millions of people around the world to celebrate 2018 Year of the Bird.

In the book entitled *When Women Were Birds: Fifty-Four Variations on Voice*, author and environmental activist Terry Tempest Williams wrote, "Once upon a time, when women were birds, there was the simple understanding that to sing at dawn and to sing at dusk was to heal the world through joy. The birds still remember what we have forgotten, that the world is meant to be celebrated." (Tempest Williams, 2012)

So, while our birds still sing, people who care all together around the world joined in the celebration of 2018 as the Year of the Bird to remember that those tuneful voices that lift us in our darkest hours are the ones that we humans are actively working to silence once again, possibly for forever. "They are our last, best connection to a natural world that is otherwise receding." (Goldberg, 2018)

In the past, people exterminated many species of birds by hunting and habitat destruction. Today, humanitarians standing against bird trafficking and awareness of bird smugglers that are hurting the natural wildlife habitat.

Now, people are standing against bird species' extinction caused by environmental degradation. The trash in bird nests tells the story. In our times, ornithologists worry that there are signs of human influence on makeup of birds' nests as they found insulation, foil, and cigarette butts. Birds are picking up pieces of colored plastic in the wild to show their social dominance to attract the females.

Let us hope that 2018 Year of the Bird will have a strong impact on this new movement to protect the wildlife and to stop exterminate more birds in the future!

Our ancestors watched birds: there are their sightings painted on the caves' walls. Birds always helped determine the seasons and predict the weather. They provide food, and birds are pollinating plants. Birds are controlling insects and dispersing seeds. They may serve as messengers for mail-carrying, and on a personal note, they are waking me up on many sunny Sunday mornings. It is important both – what birds do for the environment and what birds do for our souls!

Everybody knows, spring means birds! Birds can foretell the changing seasons by their northward and southward migrations. If someone does not have access to local meteorologist, it is okay – people still have the birds.

About 160-million years ago, the creature called Archaeopteryx had skeleton characteristics identical to small dinosaurs that lived during that same time. This creature also had toothed jaw and feathers that allowed the Archaeopteryx to move from place to place 'transporting' through branches. Some scientists believe that Archaeopteryx is the evolutionary link between dinosaurs and what today we identify as birds. Also, birds' beaks, legs, and the ability to lay eggs indicates a strong relationship between birds and reptiles. New discoveries are helping to better understand how birds evolved and how they are related to each other, from the tiny hummingbird to the towering ostrich.

In 2005, bones discovered from Antarctica' fossil gave new and very exciting facts: the skeleton of Vegavis, dated to around sixty-seven million years ago, bears traits that exist only in a modern-day duck. The new discoveries combined with more advanced methods of genetic tests suggest that the avian family tree got their start just before the asteroid strike. (Jaggard, 2018) An asteroid stroke sixty-six-millions years ago. It devastated the dinosaurs, but scientists today have proof and evidence that there were a few survivors that evolved since many millions of years of the mass extinction and begot today's birds.

Today on Earth, birds are the only creatures that have feathers. Feather define birds. Feathers, also called plumage, are responsible for birds' ability to fly, regulate birds' temperature and provide physical protection, while giving birds their shape and color. Feathers first appeared not on birds, but on dinosaurs, long before birds evolved. Some early Tyrannosaurs sported primitive look-like-feathers. Dinosaur feathers were perhaps used for insulation or tale-display. More complex feathers specialized for business of flying, and they literarily took birds to new heights. Birds have been around for more than 100 million years; and we might be able to learn a thing, or two, or three from these feathered jewels that evolved to survive the age of dinosaurs. The question is might birds survive the age of *Homo sapiens*?

"The shape of a beak tells a poignant story of each bird's evolution and survival, and helps us to understand its place in the world," writes Noah Strycker in *Birds of the Photo Ark*. For example, sparrow's sturdy triangular beak contains the power to crack seeds; while a hawk's sharp, hooked beak makes short work of prey.

Birds were not the first to evolve the head ornamentation – both dinosaurs and even more distant relatives, the pterosaurs, had them. Today, birds display an amazing variety of crowns and crests. Birds use the incredible head ornamentations to attract mates and threaten competition. Among birds, monogamy often means pairing up only for the breeding season. This is especially true among small migratory birds, like Kentucky warblers, which winter in Central and South America.

Courtship rituals may include dances, aerial displays, posturing, sound production other than voice, the offering of gifts or food, and the exhibition of breeding plumage and other sexual characteristics. Such rituals not only serve to attract a mate and establish a pair bound, but also to warn away competing members of the same species.

Some people like to watch them, other like to feed them, many enjoy the amazing unique birdsongs. What people can do for birds? Perhaps for beginning, to start with the local environmental community or the own backyard to create an inviting sanctuary for birds, where birds will come to nest, raise their families and seek shelter for the winter. Songbirds need a protective cover from potential enemies, such as cats, snakes and hawks. Birds will stay to nest during the breeding season, if there are invited places for them to nest like trees, shrubs, hedges, brambles, and even, vines. The evergreens and shrubs planted against walls and other shelter areas will protect birds from cold, wind, and rain. From strategic landscaping to 'birdscaping' activities would help to provide birds with food sources: flower nectar, grass seed-heads, fruits, berries and a diversity of plant species to attract insects; since many songbirds are insectivores. A small pond, pool or puddle would attract thirsty birds and an interesting assortment of wildlife, including frogs, toads and dragonflies.

There are various relationships between people and birds. There are farmers who are making a living by retail and wholesale of birds; buying, raising, and loving birds. Also, there are some people who are hunting or catching birds for various reasons from food for dinner to living with birds as pets.

Historically, people have understood the necessity for birds housing while under their care. Despite their straight-forward structure and uncomplicated intention, pet bird cages have transformed from simple, boxy cane and wood structures to some of the most imaginative and complicated miniature architectural configurations ever created. As time went on, and human's understanding and knowledge of better avian care and farming developments, the bird cage changed yet again to a more up-front and utilitarian design.

The early bird cages were built for the very same reason we build them today: to house birds. Cages display birds, keep them safe from predators and prevent their escape. Early cages were handmade net enclosures and simple boxes created from materials such as wood, rope, cane or bamboo. Later on, some birds of the past were even employed in simple, tiny cages to carry out very dirty and dangerous, yet highly respected work, such as 'canaries labor' in coal mines. The birds were fearlessly used to forewarn the presence of noxious gasses; if the canary fell dead off its perch, the miners would know to evacuate the mine.

The bird cage mimics a bird's roost or their home in the wild. Parrots in the wild make their homes in the hollows and cavities of trees. Birds have a natural inclination to seek a place that is enclosed. Simply put, when a cage is properly set up, a pet bird finds refuge in its cage and views it as a safe retreat to rest, relax and feel safe. The cage is regarded as the bird's home and sanctuary. A good-sized cage mimics a bird's natural behavior of leaving the roost during the day and returning at night for sleep and safety. This method of keeping birds has become a more widespread practice as quality play-stands have become commonly available. The designs became sturdier with additional bird-friendly features.

Please do not under estimate the necessity of the bird cages in modern times as 571 bird species are classified as critically endangered, and further four exist only in captivity.

Common Birds: Doves and Pigeons

There is a debate as to whether the first domesticated bird was the pigeon or the chicken, but historic evidence shows that the world's oldest domesticated bird most probably was a rock pigeon. Mesopotamian tablets mention the domestication of pigeons more than 5,000 years ago, as do Egyptian hieroglyphics. Research suggests that domestication of pigeons occurred as early as 10,000 years ago. There are various figurines, mosaics, and coins that have portrayed the domestic pigeon since at least 4500 B.C. in Mesopotamia. In many cultures, doves and pigeons have been raised as pets for thousands of years and even used as sacrifices to appease the Gods. In most religions of the world, pigeons and doves are loved and respected, and accorded a special place. Because people were hunting them for food, some of the species of doves and pigeons have either become extinct or are considered as threatened to extinct. Doves and pigeons were the only birds suitable for sacrifice by the Hebrews. (Leviticus 1:14.) The dove appears as a symbol of purity on the Holy Grail in Malory's Morte d'Arthur. In Christianity, dove has come to represent the symbol of Holy Spirit. As a symbol of the Holy Spirit, the dove is associated with the mystical fifth element of spirit. In Muslim folklore, "a dove murmured the words of God into the ear of Muhammad."

Today, the dove is a symbol of peace, often portrayed with an olive branch in its mouth. This iconography is taken from the story of Noah releasing the bird to bring back proof that there was land again somewhere and that the floodwaters were receding. The dove is the representation of love as seen by many. It was a symbol of Aphrodite, the Greek Goddess of Love; and of Venus, her Roman counterpart. Lovers are said to *"bill and coo"* like doves. The dove is a monogamous bird, which may be the source of its connection with romantic and eternal love. In Slavic folklore, doves were believed to conduct the souls of the dead to heaven. For the Celts, the mournful call of a dove meant the peaceful passing of someone.

Pigeons and doves are cute-looking small birds that are found in different parts of the world. Every country in the world except Antarctica has pigeons or doves. Since they are soft and delicate, doves and pigeons were hunted for food, and also kept as pets in homes. According to *Global Britannica*, the terms *dove,* and *pigeon* are often used interchangeably. However, there are differences between the two species. Doves typically have smaller bodies and bigger tails than pigeons. But there is an exception: the domestic pigeon, which is often called a 'rock dove' and widely known as the "dove of peace." The most popular types of doves and pigeons are band-tailed pigeon, rock pigeon, common ground-dove, white-tipped dove, white-winged dove, Inca dove, and the Eurasian collared-dove. The famous feral pigeons, also called "city doves, city pigeons, or street pigeons," are pigeons that are derived from the domestic pigeons that have returned to the wild. The wild rock pigeons, known as rock doves, renamed in 2004. Rock pigeons outlying Scottish islands, remote areas of Mediterranean, North Africa, and western Asia.

As the story goes, pigeons in North America are the feral population of the domesticated form of the Old World's Rock Dove. Pigeons were brought to the New World by early colonists for food, for pets, as a mean of communication, and for recreational racing.

Below are interesting facts about doves vs. pigeons:

- Both belong to a family of birds called *Columbidae.*
- The difference between doves and pigeons lies in their size.
- While doves are smaller in size and have a pointed tail, pigeons are larger in size and have a rounded tail.
- Both are found in almost all parts of the world.
- Pigeons can carry all sorts of dangerous diseases, some of which have been passed on to humans. That is why they have the nicknames "flying rats" and "rats with wings." This problem does not apply to doves.
- Both pigeons and doves like to eat seeds and fruits that form their staple diet. However, there are some species such as ground doves and quail doves that prey on insects and worms.
- Mourning doves are the most frequently hunted species in North America. Every year, hunters harvest more than twenty million, but the Mourning dove remains one of the most abundant birds, with the U.S.A. population estimated at 350 million.
- The oldest known Mourning dove was a male; and at least, thirty years, four months old at the time he was shot in Florida in 1998. He had been banded in Georgia in 1968.
- Because people are hunting them for food, some of the species of doves and pigeons have either become extinct or are considered as threatened. Pigeons always had been the perfect source of protein. Pigeon's flesh suitable for roasting or braising.

The reliance on pigeons for food declined when it became clear that chickens were more suited to mass production.

- There are over 300 species of doves and pigeons in the *Columbidae* family, but each type has its own unique style or sound of cooing or crooning.
- Both the male and the female of *Columbidae* species produce milk for their young. Pigeon 'milk' is a cottage cheese-like fluid secreted from lining of the crops. By the way, flamingos are the only other birds to feed their young the same way. Also, pigeon milk contains a higher level of protein and fat than the milk produced by mammals. Perhaps therefore, pigeons played an important and useful role in medicine. Prolactin, the hormone responsible for milk production in mammals, was first isolated in 1933 from pigeons.
- The coo-OOOO-woo-woo-woo call is almost always uttered by the male bird, not the female, an invitation to a mate or potential mate.
- Doves are the emblem of peace. This said, the white dove is most commonly representing purity, love and peace. It is also believed that spotting a white dove should be a reminder to be reconnected spirituality to the loved ones.

In popular culture, it was almost a war of words and attitudes for pigeons. It was the satirist Tom Lehrer who started the deterioration in 1959 with his song *Poisoning Pigeons in the Park*, which explained that it takes only a smidgen of strychnine and "it's not against any religion to want to dispose of a pigeon." However, Woody Allen delivered the coup *de grâce* in his 1980's movie *Stardust Memories*, when he referred to feral pigeons as "rats with wings." The term had first appeared in 1966 in an article in *The New York Times*, but Allen's film reached a much wider audience. It was the final nail in the coffin for these birds. What could be more critical than to be in comparing with rats? Ever since, feral pigeons have been one of the 'disgusting' species together with North American grey squirrels also known as 'tree rats.'

The rearing and racing pigeons declined in popularity as both hobbies require a great deal of patience and dedication – commodities in short supplies in the modern times.

But pigeons are probably most famous for their ability to find their way home and deliver messages. The Chinese used homing pigeons to deliver some of their mail as long ago as 1000 B.C. First exploited 3,000 years ago, and by the fifth century B.C., both Syria and Persia had widespread networks of message-carrying pigeons.

In 1850, Paul Julius Reuter's fledgling news service used homing pigeons to fly the 120 km between Aachen and Brussels, thereby laying the foundations for a global news agency. To remember and honor the event, the world's first 'airmail' stamps were issued for the *Great Barrier Pigeon-Gram Service*. But the only large-scale use of pigeons to deliver mail in modern times occurred in Paris during the 1870s. At this time, France and Prussia were at war, and the Prussians had surrounded the city of Paris. For many months, they wouldn't allow anything, including mail, to enter or leave the city. But the French found a clever way to keep their postal system working. Mail was sent to Frenchmen outside Paris by means of hot-air balloons, which also carried hundreds of homing pigeons. Letters that were sent to Paris were first reduced in size by photography, so that 30,000 letters could be carried on film placed inside a canister. These canisters were attached to pigeons, and the pigeons flew into Paris. Thirty-five pigeons carried the same letters, so that in case any were shot down, at least one would reach Paris. In Paris, the film was projected on a screen, and the letters were copied by hand and delivered to homes in the city. The mail delivery system became known as the "pigeon post!" (Hill, 2008)

The birds' 'homing' ability was harnessed in the two world wars: in the early 1940s, the American Signal Pigeon Corps consisted of 3,150 soldiers and 54,000 birds. About ninety percent of the messages got through. Also, these avian 'secret agents' saved countless lives, too.

As a result, of fifty-four Dickin Medals (the animal's VC) awarded in World War II, thirty-two honorable medals went to pigeons.

Even now, homing pigeons remain useful in means of communication in remote areas. The Police Pigeon Service in Orissa, India, was retired only in 2002. We are all captivated by the Internet, yet in 2009, as part of a public relation stunt, a pigeon carried a 4GB memory stick eighty km in South Africa. Perhaps this is the reason why Taliban banned people from keeping or using homing pigeons in Afghanistan.

The consensus is that pigeons use the sun and the Earth's magnetic field on long journeys, with visual cues becoming important near their loft, though recent studies suggest that they may also use odors. Not bad for birds with tiny brains! The modern technology is the fundamental reason that human reliance on pigeons rapidly reduced. It is no wonder that feral pigeons thrive to the urban areas. Buildings are perfect nest- sites for these exiles, mimicking the windswept cliffs used by their ancestors.

People like the interaction with feral pigeons. The charming birds continue to draw attention of tourists in 'hot sports" such as London's Trafalgar Square and Venice's San Marco Plazzo. Also, pigeons cause nuisance problems when they become too numerous in a particular site – entrances to public buildings, schools, warehouses, feedlots, etc. They perch and nest on horizontal surfaces such as eaves, gables, and ledges, and their droppings fall on the ground below. The population can be reduced by trapping and removing the birds. However, because they are homing pigeons, they cannot stay long at the captured site.

Pigeons as pets can live in both outdoor and indoor environments. Of course, they need cages; and in this case, bigger is better. Aviary cages are for birds' welfare and protection. Pigeons excel at their leisure arts and spend their time bathing, preening, lounging in the sun, foraging for favorite seeds, watching the sky, napping, showing off and courting. Every four to five weeks, mated couples will lay a pair of eggs. Pigeons are smart, easy going birds that quickly learn household routines. They do fine in homes with other pets and can live peacefully and unafraid with dogs and cats if they are kept safe. Pigeons are very emotional and do need the BFF (the best-friend-forever), whether another bird or a human with whom they can spend the day.

To proof the doves and pigeons are kind and carrying, let us turn to Aesop's fable *Ant and Dove*. An ant went to a fountain to quench his thirst and, tumbling in, was almost drowned. But a dove that happened to be sitting on a neighboring tree saw the ant's danger and, plucking off a leaf, let it drop into the water before him. The ant mounting upon it, was presently wafted safely ashore. Just at that time, a fowler was spreading his net and was in the act of enmeshing the dove, when the ant, observing his object, bit the man's heel. This made the man drop his net and the dove, aroused to a sense of it danger, flew safely away. The timeless story has a moral: one good turn deserves another. *"One act of kindness, how small is ever wasted."* (Aesop, N.d.)

ANCIENT ENCLOSURES

Over the centuries, the interest popularity of keeping birds in cages has risen, and fallen. The history of the bird cage is tied to the adoption of birds as pets. There are references to birds and cages in Bible: "Like a cage full of birds." (Jeremiah 5:27) The history of bird cages can be traced to the ancient world.

For instant, already in the eighth century B.C., an iron bird cage in a typical Greek household is mentioned by Pollux. Many ancient Greek vases depict tall wicker cages, the characteristic of craftsmanship in the fifth and fourth centuries B.C. Additional evidence of bird cages can be traced to nearly all cultures of the world. Another example: the oldest civilization of Sumerians is known to have written records where the word 'subura' was used for bird cages.

In ancient Greece, Plato recounts Socrates to compare the human mind to a bird cage during a philosophical debate in his dialogue with Theaetetus.

In the fifth century B.C., the Persian physician Ctesiphon wrote about his captive birds that they can speak in human voices and assured his readers that birds raised in Persia could learn to speak fluent Greek language.

The Babylonians, the Hindu merchants of the fifth century B.C., the Polynesians, and the Vikings known as ancient mariners that often-carried caged birds on long ocean journeys. When seeking land, they would release a bird and observe its flight. If the bird would see land, it would be disappeared, and sailors would follow in the bird's fly direction. If no land would find, the bird would return to the ship to be placed back in its cage.

When the Macedonians under the leadership of Alexander the Great reached India in 327 B.C., his Generals Nearchus and Onesicritus amused themselves by collecting native parakeets. Some say that Alexander the Great was given a parakeet by one of his general who managed to keep few birds alive by keeping them in heavy iron cages during the journey home to Greece. Prototypes of those birds are known today as *Alexandrine parakeets*.

Ancient Romans kept and held birds as well, and it was considered the duty of a slave to care for the domesticated birds and animals. By the time of the Roman Republic, there was an increasing trend toward the status to display the bird collections owned amongst the aristocracy. The role of caged-birds and their status are something that showed up in the bird cage symbolism. "From the late Republic on, there is Roman evidence for the caged-bird as a feature of domestic interior ornament in both prose and verse, in a diversity of genres, and there is also a limited amount of evidence from Roman art. This phenomenon is something new and distinctively Roman, as was the toga, the genre of verse satire." (Jones, n.d.)

The ancient Egyptians kept birds caged for their beauty and mystery nearly four centuries ago. Doves and parrots were among favorite birds of the Egyptians as they were depicted in hieroglyphics.

The early Christian sarcophagus from the Vatican cemetery has that look alike a domed bird cage with the bird sitting on top of it, signifying that the soul of the person had been liberated from its earthly prison. (Randall, 1953)

Before the Spanish ever crossed the Atlantic, an ancient people were breeding scarlet macaws. The Paquet Indians of the Pre-Columbian period at the Puebloan community built and occupied an elaborate settlement made from adobe, about 900 to 1340 A.D. What was found there by archeologists, was astounding – approximately fifty-six macaw enclosures of bird cages that were made of adobe.

Not all early cages were made in traditional cage structure manner. However, due to a paper published by the Society for American Architecture in 1993, ancient ruins were discovered in the northwest corner of the Mexican state of Chihuahua called *Casas Grandes,* associated with the remains of relatively unusual aviary. These coops were made of adobe clay, shaped and smoothed by hand. Made of the same material that was used for housing people – they resemble a rectangular flower pot with a round plug at the end. The adobe kept the resident's cooler, and the coops even contained stone doors and plugs. Researchers suggests that large-scale breeding of scarlet macaws occurred there long before the industrial age. These ancient bird breeders harvested the birds' feathers for use in their ceremonial religious rituals, a common Meso-American practice. They most likely traded these feathers with Native American societies in the southwestern area of the United States of America as well. While macaw remains have been found among some tribes of the region, it is believed that the Paquimé dominated the "parrot exchange."

An aviary, a large cage to house and display birds, is dating far back, possibly earlier than the 1500s, found in the Aztec city of Tenochtitlan as noted by Hernan Cortes; when he, and his men, arrived in Americas continent, in 1521. Hernan Cortes was a Spanish conquistador who led his expedition to the South of America continent that caused the fall of Aztec Empire.

When Western traders brought back spices and textiles from the Far East, they also brought back exotic birds as pets.

In the American colonies, birds were much beloved pets, and the colonists kept their birds in simple wooden cages.

The mynah has been considered a sacred bird in India for at least 2,000 years as well. The birds were pulled through the streets on oxen, likely in crude cages, to ensure they would not escape. It is difficult to determine what some of these cages may have been made of, perhaps local materials such as wooden twigs, rope mesh, reeds, or bamboo.

Pet Birds Developments

To follow the pet birds' developments in the bird cages in chronological order, let highlight the major timeline in history. The Gothic times include the Medieval era, approximately from twelfth century to sixteenth century. Later, followed by short period of Regency era (1811-1820), and the Victorian era named accordingly for the Queen Victoria regency (1837-1901).

As early as 1341, when Portuguese sailors visited the Canary Islands and other neighboring islands such as Azores and Madeira, they were fascinated by small noticeable birds with extraordinary voices of songs. Later, in the reign of King Manuel I (1491-1521) of Portugal, it was a tendency to keep canaries in cages. As a fact, there are various portraits of ladies of this era displayed with their beloved birds. The merchants from Portugal and Spanish vessels were selling canaries to Tuscan merchants by the weight in gold. Following in the steps of Portuguese explorer Vasco de Gama, traders began transporting parrots in large numbers from Africa, India and Java to the capitals of Europe.

Over the centuries, the interest and popularity of keeping birds in cages as pets have as people say 'waxed and waned.' Wood and wicker were the most common materials used to make bird cages in the Medieval times. The rattan cages had a pointed or rectangular shape and were simply hawked by peddlers along the streets. In 1379, iron cages were also common in the palaces of Louis XI and Isabella of Bavaria. The King of France was one of the earliest bird admires, and other European monarchs soon followed him in the fashionable trend.

The discovery of the New World stimulated the arriving of the American bird species to Europe such as South American macaws, which are larger than their cousins, the African parrots, and the yellow-headed amazon that was brought back home by Columbus.

In some of the richer mansions and palaces, cages were fashioned to complement the atmosphere of rich fashion costumes and interior design environments, gold-thread hangings, and sumptuous tableware. Gold and silver were used for the cage frames, which were richly adorned with jewels and buntings. The cages in Louis XI's salon were not only made of silver with landscapes and rural scenes painted around their bases, but they were glittered with shining crystals of cut glass that hung from their lower edges. A curious cage made for Isabella of Bavaria in 1402 had six gilded pillars spread with a netting made of golden fish scales. Also, forty years earlier, an account of Robert de Serres mentions a cage made of silver and decorated with enamel. (Randall, 1953)

Talking birds were in favor to inspire folklore. Due to Randall, old European tales tell of pet birds reporting to jealous husbands the infidelities of young wives or tattling on other doers of immoral deeds.

Royals of various regions throughout the 14th and 15th centuries frequently received exotic birds as gifts. Noblemen were reported to have carried bird companions in "travel-size" cages while on the road. The keeping of exotic birds gradually fell out of fashion over the course of the next few centuries, but it was revived in the seventeenth century.

Ornamented and structurally lavish cages of the noble classes in Europe around the 14th century were leading the trend and became the staple of their culture. Experts and collectors agree that of these early cages, the most talented artisans were the French and the Dutch. In France, a guild of cage makers was licensed and chartered by royalty to fabricate cages generally made of iron or brass wire. These guilds of artisans made cages specifically for male and female songbirds. Charles V of France had decorative bird cages made from "gold and silver filled with birds of enamel and precious metals, set with the finest gems. These minute birds were sweetly perfumed, and the cages hung in the wardrobes and chambers of the palaces as sachets." (Randall, 1953)

When in the 17th century birds became trendy once again, bird-keeping as pets was considered a chic attraction in England and France. They took a step beyond making cages merely to keep birds in them. The cages evolved to became a decorative item strictly for display. These decorative cages were often made with mahogany and brass, fitted with porcelain and silver bowls. It seems that the 'airiness' and the impact of the bird cage within the interior design added a compelling visual effect that pleased many homeowners.

At these times, all birds were in vogue and stylish for many reasons. Songbirds provided a background noise that was pleasing to the ear and many cages were designed to be carried from room to room to follow the owner. They were the first 'portable entertainment centers,' long before the transistor radio, the stereo or the iPod. The most popular exotic bird in seventeenth-century England was the *popinjay*, known to us today as the parrot. These large, colorful, often talkative birds were imported from the tropics, were difficult to obtain and, therefore, were very expensive. Only the very wealthy could afford to own a popinjay, which became a status-symbol of this historic period. But having the bird was only part of the package, to show off their prize-parrot to its best advantage, it must be displayed in a cage, which would do justice to such a valuable creature.

After the world explorer Magellan's death, Sebastian del Cano continued his expedition. It is good documented in Spain that del Cano received a colorful as 'vibrant tropical flowers' bird of paradise with a ribbonlike feathered tail as a gift from the sultan of Batjan in the Philippines. (Dennis, 2014) Upon the expedition's return to Spain in 1522, del Cano's bird created a sensation.

The fashion for keeping popinjays continued in the eighteenth century, but keeping other exotic birds also became fashionable as traders of goods from the East brought back from their trade expeditions more and more species of exotic birds along with their cargoes of spices, teas, porcelains and textiles. With the advancement of more frequent shipments, the cost of these exotic birds dropped enough to make them available not just to wealthy aristocrats, but also to the more affluent among the upper bourgeoisie class. Only few among the middle or lower classes would have been able to afford even one of these exotic birds, they were simply too expensive.

Changing consumer practices in the eighteenth century were led by the Middle class. Parrots remained a status-symbol in the eighteenth century, and there were nearly as many parrots kept in the eighteenth century as there had been in the seventeenth century. But love-birds, doves and several species of songbirds had also become popular. Ladies, in particular, preferred the softer, sweeter sounds of songbirds to the often raucous and strident calls of parrots. Unlike parrots, songbirds were usually kept in pairs or in family groups and their singing was soothing and pleasing to the ear. In fact, caged songbirds were providing background music. In some French gardens, to enhance an *al fresco* entertainment, several cages of songbirds were covered with foliage and hung in the trees to provide 'natural' music. Though less common in England, there were a few *al fresco* entertainments at which guests were serenaded by songbirds as they strolled through the garden of their grand estate.

In the 18th century, birds lived in dwellings that were more reminiscent of houses for people than for the birds themselves. Birds, especially songbirds, were quite popular, and very much in fashion among the very rich. Often made of expensive and exotic woods, and built like miniature architectural models, these structures were found among the very rich and fashionable people of England and France. The birds in cages might have reflected on the design of real buildings and perhaps were models of 'what could be' in the mind of the cage architects. While structurally beautiful, most of these fantastic cages did little to support the needs of the bird. Often dangerous for the birds and difficult to clean, it's amazing that the birds survived in these structures at all. They were often painted and constructed with lead-based (Pb) materials and had exposed to nail-heads. Were these birdcages beautiful? Yes. Were these birdcages practical? No.

Keeping pet birds was so popular during this time that mechanical cages became all the rage. These novelty trinkets became even more popular during the Victorian era, when a trendy wedding gift was a gilded cage with a mechanical bird that flapped its wings, sang and hopped about. It was the blender of its era!

At the same time, in other areas of the world, cages were being built out of bamboo, wicker, wood, rattan and reed. Early examples of cage-work made by the Chinese artisans had been fabricated in the 18th century. These unique exotic models were simple in design and unadorned, but were aesthetically pleasing and made with beautiful authentic materials.

In Tunisia, a small country in Northern Africa, they uphold a long-standing tradition of constructing ornately domed bird cages – the craft had been passed down paternally, from one generation to another.

Decorative bird cages for sale could be costing thousands. Some are gilded in gold or covered in hand carved designs of wood, silver, or gold and other precious metals. These cages are also could be found as antiques entities of the Victorian era. Finding decorative bird cages today for collectors could be difficult. Antique stores or online vendors are the best sources.

Cockatoo bird cages and those for other large parrots can often be larger than most furniture in the room. Because of them, manufacturers have some models that may have beautiful decorations and bases made of hand crafted wood trims. In some cultures, a bird cage represents captivity or entrapment. Most cultures, though, see decorative bird cages as wonderful works-of-art. Many cages are designed to fit the traditions of the region where they were made. An oriental cage may have architecture similar to the ancient oriental buildings, or Tuscan cages could do the same and use the architecture of iconic Italian buildings.

Well over a century before the Regency period began, both the exotic birds and their cages had become a staple feature of interior decor for several bird aficionados of the upper classes. Many those cages were extremely elaborate and represented the flamboyant architectural confections. Quite a few of them remained in the families of their original owners for many generations, so they might still have been in use during the Regency period.

At the Regency time, birds were less often kept as status-symbols and were more often kept as pets by those who admired their beauty and were fascinated by their behavior. For example, Lord Byron loved the macaw he kept in his rooms at Albany and refused to remove him, despite repeated complaints from his neighbors about the bird's loud and raucous calls.

It must be noted that though the existence of the *budgerigar*, known more commonly in England as the 'budgie,' and as the *parakeet* in America, was first recorded in 1805, it did not become a common household pet until the Victorian era. Also, it is extremely doubtful that there was a single budgie housed in a bird cage anywhere in England during the Regency period.

By the Victorian era, the bird was considered even more than a pet. The decorative cage was an important ornamentation within the Victorian parlor. They became even more cherished and loved by the higher classes of the aristocratic society. Considered exotic, rare and difficult to obtain, parrots were the chosen bird to demonstrate how fashionable and wealthy the household was. Fewer accounts exist for the average household, but we know that among the possessions of the poor goldsmith John Cobham of York there was a bird cage valued at one penny. (Randall, 1953) Most of these cages were made with a strong bent iron frame in Gothic architectural designs similar the designs, which were used in the construction of Gothic cathedrals and palaces. Finer wire mesh was placed inside the wrought iron framework to contain smaller birds.

Gentlemen, especially lonely unsocial scholars, often enjoyed the company of a parrot, teaching the bird to talk and allowing them to run free in their study or book-room during the day. Ladies tended to prefer love-birds, doves and song birds as pets, because they were entranced by the strong bond between birds, which mated for life. In addition, they enjoyed the more delicate appearance and softer voices of these smaller birds, which were also somewhat less expensive to acquire and maintain.

In nineteenth century, the styles and designs of bird housing evolved and morphed from simple, rustic-looking boxes – to wild, wonderful, and sometimes showy architectural structures. These rustic bird cages were often made with sturdy twigs and other natural materials, or they were made of wire or woven wood strips, and then embellished with natural-looking materials. Small sections of turf were less frequently employed to line the floors of eighteenth-century bird cages and sand or fine soil was more often used as a floor cover. Unlike in modern times, newspapers were quite expensive and were not normally used to line the bottoms of bird cages.

Also, canaries were mentioned as pets from 1796, including the *Ode to a Canary* and *Elegiac Stomas on the Untimely Death of a Young Lady's Favorite Canary Bird.* (Waldock, 2014) Both canaries and finches seem to have been among the most popular pet birds for those of the less affluent classes during the Regency period.

When people hear the word 'canary,' they probably think of a cheery, bright yellow birds. While this image is by no means inaccurate, canaries come in a wide variety of colors, patterns, and shapes. Canaries continue to be very popular pets because they are very beautiful, and the males of the species sing lovely songs.

Amazingly, the cages that have survived time and tell the story of these eras are still coveted to this day. Because these rustic cages were made of perishable materials, not many survived the ages, which makes them valuable and collectible.

In modern days, collectors often seek bird cages of a certain style or period. Jon Douglas, co-owner of *Figs Home & Garden* in Phoenix, has been collecting them for approximately fifteen years. He has about thirty vintage and antique ones in his personal collection and an untold number for sale in his store. His favorite styles hail from East Asia and Europe from the 1900s.

Derived the 19th century, bird cages began to shift from functional to architectural eye-candy. Many of these cages were built to represent monumental buildings, such as the Taj Mahal, the Eiffel Tower or a Georgian mansion. At one point, parrots were only housed in these fanciful cages to roost. During the day, they applied their time on T-stands or circular perches nearby.

Before the late 20th century, little was known about the physical needs of birds. Regarded as little more than 'décor' to liven up the household, birds added distinction to the families that owned them.

At the beginning of the 20th century, bird cage manufacturers such as *Hendryx*, and *Jewett* stepped up their manufacturing to keep up with the popular canary and budgerigar market by producing painted tin cages. The *Andrew B. Hendryx Company* was founded in 1874 in Ansonia, Connecticut, under the name of *Hendryx & Bartholomew*, and at this time, produced fourteen different styles of brass bird cages. Five years later, the company moved to its ultimate location at 86 Audubon Street in New Haven, Connecticut, and changed its name to the *Andrew B. Hendryx Company*. A publication from 1904, stated that the company manufactured *"350 different styles and sizes of brass, bronze, and japanned bird and animal cages; and in addition, complete lines of fishing reels, artificial baits, chains and wire picture cord."* Much of Hendryx's success was due to his patented inventions and improved methods of manufacturing. Producing numerous bird cage designs, the company also manufactured small animal cages. Hendryx produced an annual catalog, and the goods were distributed all over the United States of America and Canada, and exported to almost every country in the world.

Hendryx died in 1910, and the company was taken over by his son, Nathan. Into the latter half of the 20th century, the company became obsolete, and sold its assets to the Chicago-based *Prevue Metal Products*. A conscious decision was made to preserve the Hendryx name. In December of 1996 the last remnants of the New Haven plant were sold at a two-day auction, marking an end to a legendary era of bird cage manufacturing in America.

The brass bird cage stood alone on the floor rather than being placed on a table or hung from the ceiling. As cage design progressed, these wire cages that hung on a stand became popular for years in both round and square versions. Now, due to a better understanding of a bird's need for feeling secure, round cages are rarely manufactured in the United States of America. Birds appreciate the security of a wall or solid structure behind them. Their survival instinct makes them cautious, always seeking a safe place to perch. A solid structure behind them affords them the knowledge that nothing can sneak up behind them.

Later, plastic cages became the trend with the approach toward practicality, utility and function rather than aesthetic concerns. However, it has been generally accepted that the durability and life-use of these cages is limited.

To move up with the theme the history-of-pet-birds-cages, below are listed the definitions and facts for the subject matter.

- Avian aka bird, avian is everything associated with birds.
- Aviary – a large enclosure for confining birds. Unlike *cages*, aviaries allow birds a larger living space where they can fly. Aviaries are also sometimes known as *flight cages*. Aviaries often contain plants and shrubbery to simulate a natural environment.

The *Raven Cage* build in 1829, is regarded as one of the oldest structures in the London Zoo.

The *Birds of Eden* bird sanctuary, located in the Western Cape of South Africa, is possibly the largest free flight aviary in the world. The aviary opened in 2005 and covers an area of 234,230 sq. ft. It is home to around 3,000 individual birds from 200 species.

Miami Metro Zoo in Florida, USA, has an aviary with many different birds that walk among guests attending the zoo.

- Bird cage or birdcage – also known as cage, chicken coop, hen house, pet, and aviary.
- Coop – meaning enclosed, surrounded, or fenced area.
- Pet – meaning domesticated, in household.
- Plumage – feathers, fluff and fuzz.

Interesting Facts: The large enclose of birds gave the name to a street in London. The *Birdcage Walk* is a street in the city of Westminster. The street is named after the Royal Menagerie and Aviary, which were located there in the reign of King James I. Later, King Charles II expanded the Aviary. Samuel Pepys and John Evelyn both mention visiting the Aviary in their diaries.

The question is what were the most desirable birds? Linnets, thrushes, nightingales, European robins, bullfinches, goldfinches, purple finches, mockingbirds, cardinals, but by far the most popular was the canary. Small neighborhood stores were as common in 19th-century cities and towns in America as were barbershops. As a fact, sometimes, barbershops were selling birds too.

There is a lot of information about two brothers named Charles and Henry Reiche. It looks that these two brothers, who immigrated from Germany in 1843, were the most successful bird dealers in America. The Bird shop in Manhattan at 55 Chatham Street near Bowery operated by importing birds and selling about two thousand canaries a year. Reiche brothers scored a windfall by shipping three thousand canaries a year to California during the California's Gold

Rush. In 1853, Charles Reiche published a book entitled *The Bird Fancier's Companion*. The book became immediately popular and was reprinted many times. Since 1853 to 1867, Reiches imported about twenty thousand canaries each year. In 1871, the number increased to forty-eight thousand of birds.

Birds and Cages

Bird-Catching and Bird-Watching Traditions

"A forest bird never wants a cage." (Henrik Ibsen)

Knowledge about the birds' behavior was collected and passed down over centuries and generations. For example, hunting with falcons is a tradition that goes back millennia in Arabic culture. 'Falconry' in Asia dates back to at least to 1000 BC. For the Asian prairie countries such as Mongolia and Kazakhstan, hunting with golden eagles on horseback is still part of everyday life in some nomadic tribes.

Also, there is one of the oldest traditions: bird catching by bird-catchers. A bird-catcher is someone who catches or ensnares birds. In the United States, people talk about "going hunting where the ducks are," so people can hunt ducks and other fowl such as wild turkeys or pheasants, because people will be going to shoot them dead. Bird trapping techniques to capture wild birds include a wide range of techniques that have their origins in the hunting of birds for food. While hunting for food does not require birds to be caught alive, some trapping techniques capture birds without harming them and are successfully in use in ornithology research.

Someone who 'hunts' would be a 'hunter.' The terms 'fowler' or bird-catcher are used in bird-catching alive ancient tradition. Besides, bird-catcher is an old occupation, as the people made a living by catching birds for sell. Also, the bird-boy is an old occupation too, as people employed boys to scare away birds from crops. (*Obscure Old English Census Occupations*, 2012)

Local geographical traditions have a long history. For example, the tradition of bird-catching in the Salzkammergut, tourist region in Austria, includes the catching of individual local forest birds in the late fall. The caught birds would be kept outside during the fowling season in aviaries at the forest bird exhibition; than on the Sunday, before St. Catherine's Day, the 25th of November, the most beautiful birds would be exhibited and awarded. In spring the birds would be released into the wild again. Bird-catching Christmas native scenes and stories documented in the region's songs and poems.

The Greek fables have a long history related to birds in captivity. Below is a short fable entitling *The Caged Bird and the Bat:*

> A singing bird was confined in a cage, which hung outside a window. The bird filled the night with beautiful songs, while all the other birds were asleep. One night a bat came and clung to the bars of the cage, and asked the bird why she was silent by day and only sang by night. "I have a very good reason for doing so," said the bird. "It was once when I was singing in the daytime that a fowler was attracted by my voice, and he netted for me and caught me. Since then I have never sung, except by night." The bat replied, "It is no use singing at night now when you

are already a prisoner. If only you had done so before you were caught, you might still be free."

The bird-catcher or fowler and the Blackbird were the main characters of one of *Aesop's Fables*, numbered 193 in the *Perry Index*. The fable entitled "*The Bird-Catcher and The Lark:*"

> A bird-catcher had set up his snare for the birds. A lark observed these preparations and asked the bird-catcher what he was doing. The man said to the lark that he was founding a city. The man then moved away from the snare. The bird, believing what the man had said, approached and ate some of the bait. Then, without realizing it, he was trapped in the snare. As the bird-catcher ran up and grabbed hold of the lark, the bird said to him, "Look here, if this is the sort of city you are founding, you won't find many inhabitants for it!"

Modern European retellings of the fable include Giovanni Maria Verdizotti's 1570 version, which has a lark as the bird. The nearly contemporary French edition of 1582, however, features a blackbird; and it is followed in Roger L'Estrange's 1692 collection. An alternative tradition dating back to the *Greek Anthology* states that the blackbird is under the special protection of the Gods, and cannot be trapped in nets.

The famous François Boucher (French artist, 1703 - 1770) *The Bird Catchers* painting of 1748 was made in oil on canvas responding to the contemporary rage for pastorals depicting amorous countryside games. François Boucher skillfully exhibited young, fashionable couples in the act of catching birds. In the 1700s, small birds played an important symbolic role in courtship ritual: the gift of a caged bird from a man to a woman signified her capture of his heart. Posed in front of the ruins of a temple to Vesta, young aristocratic women dressed in exquisite finery play with small birds; some still hold them on strings, while others daintily hold them on their fingers.

The Bird Catchers and *The Fountain of Love* were finished models for a series of tapestries known as the *Noble Pastorales*. Eventually, they were cut up into sections and sold separately. The tapestries reveal how large the cartoons or models originally were, and how much is missing from the cut-up sections.

Birdcatcher Fowler painting, 1870. Oil on canvas.
Vasily Perov (Russian artist, 1834-1882) Gender: real-life realism

The Fowler and the boy both are watching and are ready in the position to catch a bird. There are two bird cages in the painting's seen. One is covered with a cloth to keep the caught bird or birds quiet. The boy has a second cage; he is all focused, with the eyes on the bird. The old man, the Fowler, lays silently. His left hand has a string of the trap and the other hand helps to make the sound to allure the desired bird.

The classic music *The Bird Catcher's Aria* from Wolfgang Amadeus Mozart's opera "The Magic Flute" pays the music acknowledgement to the ancient skill and tradition. "The Magic Flute," in German language: *Die Zauberflöte*, is an opera in two acts by Wolfgang Amadeus Mozart to a German libretto by Emanuel Schikaneder. The work is in the form of a *Singspiel*, a popular form that included both singing and spoken dialogue. The work premiered in 1791 at Schikaneder's theatre, in Vienna, Austria.

The opening aria for the jolly bird-catcher Papageno is entitled *"Der Vogelfänger bin ich ja,"* which may be roughly translated from German language as *"I am the bird catcher, yes."* In opera, Papageno enters wearing his costume of feathers and with a birdcage strapped to his back. He holds with both hands a pan pipe, which he plays before and during the song. He sings cheerfully of the pleasures of catching birds, but muses that it would be nice to be able to catch pretty girls too, and to make the one he liked best his wife.

There is a bronze statue entitled *Papageno with His Pan Pipes* that was sculpted by the Belgian artist Jef Claerhout in one of the best preserved ancient Medieval cities of Europe. In the statue Papageno's costume has a bird's head and wings, and his bird cage is a small hand-held version; and he is holding three captured birds in the bird cage. The statue located in front of the *City Theatre* in Bruges, Belgium.

First and foremost, it is never acceptable to catch a wild bird from its natural habitat and keep it in the zoo or in a bird cage, unless the bird is injured or incapable of surviving in the wild. Technically, catching a healthy wild bird is like kidnapping or stealing. Not only does it stress the bird; it also results in the decline of the population of the avian species.

For the sake of saving the birds, people should not take them out of their natural habitat to make them somebody's pets. Also, people should not ever support those who sales or purchase these "stolen" creatures. These days, many wild winged species are held captive in homes. So, if someone wish to have a pet, people might want to consider to adopt one that is used to live with humans. In case someone sees a sick or injured wild bird, the best would be to call animal rescuers or go to the nearest nature center for professional help.

If someone decides to keep birds that have been raised as pets and later to set them free, is it save for birds? The most common answer is "set them free." But if the bird breeders would be asked the same question, they would rather keep them. Why? The answer is simple. Birds that have been used to being with humans may not already be accustomed to living in the wild. They might find it hard to deal with the weather. Also, they don't know how to forage for food. They cannot even protect themselves from predators. That only means, if someone would set them free, it might likely would be punish them to death.

Common knowledge is that most bird species raised as pets are intelligent. Once birds bond with humans, they form a strong tie. Therefore, sending them away will only cause them anxiety and grief.

"I wish I were a tiny bird
Like the one upon that tree.
Its merry song from morn till night
Makes me dance and feel so bright."
("I Wish I Were a Tiny Bird":
[Chinese song], 2008-2013)

It is important to understand that because birds are so widespread and so visible – unlike most other vertebrates – people have observed and studied them for centuries. The earliest students of birds and birds' behaviors probably were bird hunters and bird-catchers whose interest in learning their habits was to obtain them and their eggs for various reasons: for food, for pets, and for ornamentation and clothing. The abundant of the early information on the natural history of birds was recorded by bird-catchers. Oologists are people who collected eggs as a hobby in the 1800s and in early years of this century oologist scientists are learning the birds' habitations. Today, to collect wild birds' eggs is illegal. Biologists study birds as subjects of research in anatomy, physiology, endocrinology, evolution, behavior, and ecology. In 1883, the American Ornithologists' Union has been on track to unite professional scientists in North America and even published a quarterly journal entitled *The Auk*.

Today, for instance, in Florida there are several institutions of higher education that offer educational programs in Ornithology by leading toward undergraduate and advanced degrees in biology, wild ecology, and zoology. These include the University of Florida in Gainesville, Florida State University in Tallahassee, Florida Atlantic University in Boca Raton, University of Central Florida in Orlando, University of South Florida in Tampa, the University of Miami in Coral Gables, and the Florida Institute of Technology in Melbourne. Most of these universities also maintain research collections of bird skins, skeletons, and eggs. The Florida Museum of Natural History (FMNH) in Gainesville, Florida, houses one of the top collections of bird sounds, both songs and calls, in North America.

Sometimes, in the study of birds, it is desirable or necessary to be able to identify each individual bird in the avian population. This is happening by placing a numbered band on one bird's leg, so that the bird-collected information can be observed and recorded the next time, if is captured, or, with the use of additional colored bands, researchers may be able to identify marked individuals without the need to physically recapture them. The study technique is called 'bird banding' in United States or 'bird ringing' in Europe. In North America the banding program is administrated by the United States Fish & Wildlife Service (USF & WS). Over the years the banding program has been contributed to the knowledge about the migration habits of birds, including traveled distances, directions and routes, wintering and breeding sites (also, fidelity), and age and longevity. For example, the first clue about where Chimney Swifts wintered in South America came from Indians' observation in the high Andes wearing necklaces made of bird bands.

Birds occur in almost every habitat on earth, in cities as well as in fields and forests. In historic times, the term birding meant bird hunting for food or bird keeping in cages; but today, it means the art of watching birds. Birding became a major activity. Some people prefer the term bird watching to birding. Bird enthusiasts always observe birds in their own backyard and in local neighborhood. For example, every Florida town is home to an array of species such as northern mockingbird, northern cardinal, blue jay, mourning dove, red-bellied woodpecker, common grackle, and ever-present domestic pigeon, European starling, and house sparrow, just to mention a few of the many common species. Regionally, state, national parks, and national wildlife refuges are easily accessible. Inlets and bays attract large numbers and varieties of birds. For instance, the narrow peninsula at Cape May, New Jersey, acts as a bird funnel, bringing in songbirds during their spring and fall migrations. At dawn on a good day, legendary Higbee Beach offers front-row seats to a feathered 'fashion show.' As a steady procession flies by, each bird intent to find a place to rest as birds encounter the natural barrier of Delaware Bay. With a little luck, it could be seen about twenty different species of warblers, each in its own colorful costume. Unforgettable nature's scenery!

People know that Florida has been called a tropical peninsula attached to a temperate continent. Florida is naturally divided into three regions: Panhandle, Peninsula, and the Keys. Bird-searching for Florida's bird species not difficult. Birding in the Florida Everglades National Park is some of the best places where it might be seen as many as 300 bird species. The best birding season is from December to March. That is the winter dry season when birdlife concentrates mostly around the permanent bodies of water, which makes quite easy to observe the birds in the wild life habitat. The opinion is that this is by far the best time of year for birding. Even the mosquitoes are at their least bothersome.

- Everglades Facts: Each year over a million people visit Everglades National Park, the second largest national park in the United States, after Yellowstone. The main park entrance is about an hour south of Miami, near Homestead.

In Florida, resident winter birds arrive somewhere between September to November. Among them are painted buntings of hummingbirds and blue-gray gnatcatchers, several species of warblers, sharp-shinned hawks, kestrels, peregrine falcons, and even bald eagles. Florida bald eagles begin to nest in October. In April, they and their youngsters fly to the Chesapeake Bay for the summer.

And by the way, falconry is the most highly regulated sporting activity in the United States. In the states, where falconry is legal, with exception of Hawaii, aspiring falconers have to be sponsored by an experienced falconer, then take an exam and build a safe structure to house their hawk. In addition, they have to serve an apprenticeship, at least two years, under the guidance of their sponsor.

Today, the future of bird development and surviving depend upon scientists and researchers' data who study birds. The bird-watching process of bird observation is delicate. Therefore, sunrise and sunset times change with location; and scientists have to fallow the birds in their migration journeys to be able to answer all the questions about various of species of birds and to analyze the path of each bird has taken.

In the past, Aristotle believed that some birds hibernated or transformed into other species. In medieval Europe the explanation for the appearance of barnacle geese in the winter was that they grew on trees. And one English minister theorized in the 17th century that birds flew to the moon during their migration process. In the modern times, since bird-watchers have uncovered the migrations of thousands of avian species as they move from one habitat to another with the of seasons. The birds have no choice but to travel to places where food for surviving is plentiful. Here is a fascinated story discovered by Jan van Gils, a marine ecologist from Royal Netherlands Institute for Sea Research. The red knot flies thousands of miles south for winter – to be able to stick its bill in the mud to find mollusks. Jan van Gils and his colleagues were puzzled by their observation that some of the birds are eating sea grass. Why and when they become vegetarian? By bird-watching, the researchers found that these red knots were juveniles, with shorter bills and smaller bodies. They also established that their body size various significantly by year. They were born at the time, when the temperature in Arctic was warmer, and these birds did not have enough to eat as chicks because the snow melted earlier than usual and robbed the newborns population of nutrition. After the birds migrated, their bodies were smaller, and their bills were shorter. Their bills could not reach deep in the mud to find mollusks. Sea grass is a poor source of nutrients, but they were eating it, because they did not have a choice. (Bhattacharjee, 2018)

The red knot story is just one example how the bird-watchers' research helps to understand the climate change and environmental damage that may be harming migratory species of birds. Birds often competing with industrial developments to build ports, factories, and housing. Similarly, illegal hunting and changes in land use have imperiled bird migration between Europe and Africa, and between North and South America. The industrialization of farming left migrating birds struggling to find food.

It was not until 2008 that locals of Hawaiian Islands realized that their beautiful colorful bird named iiwi declined in population. Iiwi is vulnerable and potentially, at risk. Native to North America, the iiwi prefers subtropical and tropical forest habitats. Like so many island species, the iiwi is adapted to the plants that share its evolutionary history. This small bird has vibrant red plumage overall, with black wings and tail. The salmon-colored bill is a beauty, long and decurved. It feeds primarily on nectar, but also does not avoid insects and spiders as well. Males are slightly larger than females. These birds prefer to keep hidden among the leaves. Scientists and researchers wanted to know what is causing their decline. Of course, the usual suspect such as habitat loss, but also it was discovered that the birds are very susceptible to diseases such as avian malaria, avian influenza, and fowl pox. Luckily, these beautiful birds were able to escape some of these diseases by heading into higher elevations, where they were able to escape mosquitoes, who cared the deadly bird virus. Bird watchers found large colonies of birds at the islands of Hawaii, Maui, and Kauai, common in wet forests at high elevations. There are fewer than fifty individuals on the lower elevation islands of Oahu and Molokai, and, sadly, they are now extinct from the island of Lanai.

What happened? Natural forests were replaced with farms, plantations, and towns. What was done so far to save the birds: on Moloka'i, the Nature Conservancy preserved habitat by fencing off areas within several nature reserves to keep out goats, deer and pig populations. Today, it is known that pigs create wallows, which served as incubator sites for mosquito maggots, and which in turn, spread the avian malaria.

The time is ticking, and the unique iiwi birds should be protected and saved for the generations to come from extinction that the "happy voice of the damp forest" continues the "sweet lei mamo" of the iiwi bird. (Huelani, n.d.) The yellow feathers iiwi birds are highly prized and loved by Hawaiians.

According to Worldwatch Institute, many bird populations are currently declining worldwide, with 1,200 species facing extinction in the next century. The conservation efforts are essential for birds.

As for the iiwi, they are focused mainly on habitat restoration and disease control. A number of protected areas have been established in the native highland forests. Efforts have also been underway to eliminate the mammal-predators, to control alien plants, and to restore native forest. Continuing population growth is monitored and will also be needed, along with efforts to control malaria and avian pox, and further research into the iiwi's reproductive biology.

The time of bird-catchers is in the past, the bird-watchers are the one who shape the conservation labors. The scientific community is in the best hopes that birds' numbers will increase enough that they will no longer be considered endangered to the world.

In the United States, the American Bird Conservatory's mission is to save native birds and their habitats throughout the Americas. Their commitment to bird conservation remains absolute, even while some other groups shift their mission to prioritize people over wildlife. They believe unequivocally that conserving birds and their habitats benefits all other species — including people.

"More than forty-six million Americans say that watch birds, and fifty-seven percent of Americans drink coffee daily. That means there may be more than 25 million coffee-drinking bird watchers." (Axelson, 2016) How these facts are connected? The answer is simple – by habitat. There are new world perspective and strategic understanding about the importance of shade-growing coffee production that in the same time is bird-friendly as well. There is a new world commitment to grow coffee without ago-chemicals, with reverence for birds, people, water, and environment. *Bird Friendly Coffee* brand is grown of farm certified by scientists from Smithsonian Migration Bird Center, and this factually is demonstrating mature nature canopy cover and the type of forest in which the coffee is grown. This coffee is guaranteed to support bird habitat. So, any time someone enjoys an afternoon *pintado*, coffee with a splash of milk or *tinto*, the black coffee, it is ensured that shade-growing Colombian coffee is sustaining both songbirds and people.

Step Forward for Pet Birds

Everybody met people who disapprove pet friend companionship. Well, honestly, it is not that they do not like someone's pets. Perhaps, they are just questioning whether keeping birds as pets is acceptable. There are plenty of talks – saying that keeping birds as pets is cruel because they should be set free. People say birds do not belong in our homes, especially in bird cages. The truth is, it is a matter of knowing what could be done to help birds to live a safe and sustainable life.

As people learn more about avian medicine and nutrition, they became more informed about birds' cognitive needs: their need for a large, clean environment, toys, room to move, play, flutter their wings, stretch their legs, and opportunities for social interaction. As this knowledge increases and become more widely known, the cage design follows to suit.

Cages reflect to the needs of the birds rather than the interior decorating requirements of the household. Modern designs morphed and moved seemingly backward in time to the original simple designs that are easy to clean and maintain, yet manufactured with modern materials. Ann Brooks, founder of *Phoenix Landing,* a nonprofit avian welfare organization, suggested that 'the bigger the cage, the happier the bird.'

For domestic birds, having cage-homes means to protect them from other animals and from getting into trouble. They can get into trouble easily by unattended dog or cat. Bird proofing a house is very difficult with things like ceiling fans, fireplaces, and so on. It is never a good idea to leave any bird uncaged for long period of time by day or night; especially, when people are sleeping.

Few years ago, the chicken egg prices got sky-rocketing high. Many consumers assumed because of storage, transportation, or electricity cost. No, the reason was the chicken coops that were too small and overpopulated that made chickens step over each other, creating hoax, broken legs; and even, death of the hens.

Bird cages are homes for domesticated birds. Birds require a house in which they can fly and have some freedom, but still ensures they do not fly away. Bird cages are constructed to be large enough to accommodate the motion and daily activities of domesticated birds. Cages are generally constructed of wire mesh. Some manufacturers flatten the mesh and others leave the wire round just as it is, obtained from the manufacturer. Cages constructed with mesh are carefully welded in a grid that will not permit a bird to put his or her head through the mesh to be strangled. The mesh is generally 1.5 × 1 in (3.8 × 2.5 cm) in grid. Even larger birds such as parrots are rarely put into cages with mesh larger than 1 × 1 in (2.5 × 2.5 cm).

The design of bird cages is varied. Some cages that hold one or two small domesticated birds are rectangular or square. Very popular are polygonal cages that could be quite decorative. Some cages have plastic or metal trays underneath the mesh cage without a bottom, that the cleaning of the cage only entails the detaching of the tray. Others have seed catching trays that are far wider than the cage so that the tray catches all stray seeds dropped by the bird. The basic style includes:

- Flight cages - Also known as aviaries. These cages are large in either width or height to encourage birds to move around. For a finch, for example, thickness is more important, since they tend to flit from side to side;
- Dome-top cages - As the name implies, these cages boast an expanded, curved top section that is opposed to the traditional box shape. The extra interior space in these cages is great for active birds who like to climb or fly. It is also an easy way to offer the multiple birds a little more head room without sacrificing more floor space in the house;
- Play-top cages – These are made for active birds who spend large amount of time outside of their home. These are an excellent choice for birds. Many models even boast a built-in play-top that allows the birds out-of-cage time to play and interact with the family. It is also a cage-coordinated playland that easily sits on the otherwise wasted space above the cage;
- Classic cages - Whether short and squat or tall and long, these boxy cages are full of both function and style. Similar to the flight cages, but more proportionated in overall size. The classic cages comfortably suit most of any birds and often suit the owners of bird cages with an affordable price.

Still there are other cages that specifically made to breed birds and are of a very different configuration. These bird-breeding cages are quite wide with a divider in the middle that could be removed when the birds in each half of the cage have gotten used to the presence of the other. Bird-breeding cages are often made to the specifications of breeders and are designed with the recommendations collected after the bird-breeding observation and feedback from the breeders.

Untamed birds, which are not allowed out of their cages regularly, such as most finches and canaries, require larger cages that are long enough to permit some flight. The bars of these cages are spaced so that curious birds cannot stick their heads out of the cage and become stuck. The cage should also have non-toxic paint, because birds tend to gnaw at the cage, and if the paint is consumed, they can die from poisoning.

At the present time, the future for American bird cage manufacturing is a bit cloudy. The pet stores offer variety of bird cages. Large-bird discount houses are made in the countries, where labor cost is about one-tenth of labor cost in the United States. The result is that the foreign product is often cheaper than the American product. Many manufacturers and consumers agree that the imported products are far less sturdy and may not pay attention to issues such as excessive galvanization, which may be harmful to birds. American manufacturers have declined in the last several years and many are cautious with their ability to compete with inexpensive imports.

However, a local artisan from southeast industrial district of Portland, Joe Diemer, has his metalworking shop where he makes handcrafted fantasy bird cages and other metalwork wire goods. His aesthetic is elaborate and curved, referencing long-gone eras and cultures. Joe is a master of jewelry quality bird cages made from stainless steel, copper, and other beautiful materials, with the goal of reviving ornamental bird cage art for the modern home.

There are many other factors beside the bird cages that could help to be a better 'birder.' Knowledge of geography and an understanding of birds' habitats, ecology, and even weather enriches the birding experience.

For example, South Florida ecosystem is unique
in the wildlife and other habitats.

The local Tropical Audubon Society (TAS) protects natural resources in Miami-Dade and Monroe – at Biscayne Bay, Florida Bay, and the Everglades; and raises it voice against illegal bird trafficking. The United States Department of Agriculture reports that 25,000 of birds are smuggled into the USA from Central America, South America, and Mexico. Smuggled birds expose a treat to American caged birds and poultry industry. If the smuggled birds do not die from illness or stress, they often are bird-disease carriers. *It's like drugs –there is a demand. People want to have beautiful birds. Traffickers go to great lengths to conceal and transport the coveted birds, and are sometimes caught with eggs or small birds crammed into medicine tubes and hidden within their clothing."* (Iñigo-Elias, 2012) The most at-risk birds are those with colorful plumage or musical songs. Parrots are at the top of the list – part of the reason why a third of parrot species are threatened in the wild.

Often the birds have been snared in traps. Some are perished while being smuggled across the border in the caged-bird trade. Others are killed and made into accessories or talismans. For instant, hummingbirds in Mexico are killed to be sold in some markets as good luck charms for young lovers. The dry birds called *chuparosas* are difficult to accept without getting emotional. (Zuckerman, 2018).

A California man was arrested after wildlife authorities found 126 dead raptors. It's likely the biggest single case of raptors poaching in California history. The local red-tail hawks population may take years to recover from these killings. (Spillman, 2018).

Tragically, as a declining bird species gains legal protection, it becomes more valued in under-the-table transactions. Federal law in United States of America limits possession of eagle feathers and other birds' parts to the enrolled members of federally recognized tribes who use them in religious practices. It is a fact that for some tribal members, eagle feathers are essential to spiritual well-being, but to hunt them generally are remaining illegal. In most cases, it is not about spiritual well-being; it is all about greed.

Birds are meant to fly and be with others of their own kind in a natural environment! Birds bred in captivity do not fare much better. Birds older than eight to ten weeks of age do not sell well at pet shops. Many birds are kept for breeding and condemned to small cages for the rest of their lives.

Metaphoric Symbolism

The focus of this chapter is primarily how people use the bird cage motif across many human cultures. The bird in a cage is quite explicit symbol. This symbol contains two other symbols – bird and cage itself, and these two combined create a new meaning all of its own.

Birds, with their ability to fly, are often symbolize freedom. They are also related to inspiration and creativity, as being at one with the element of air. When put in a cage, the obvious symbol of a bird in cage means that freedom is lost. However, bird cages' meaning is more complex. There are more ambiguous relationships between freedom and cages. No argument that they restrain freedom – free move and actions, and hold back the birds' natural abilities to fly; but cages also protect and shield birds from danger. Therefore, to be caged may not always be a bad thing, as long as the tradeoff is worth it. Women may have felt 'caged' at home after having a new baby, but this is a time of young mom's vulnerability, and so is taking care of a newborn baby; or older parents, so the protection is certainly a worthwhile thing. Commitments to love relationships, family, new job or creative endeavor are tradeoffs on expense of free time.

Depending on the situation, the other question arises. Does the bird in the cage afraid to fly? This may be a sign of fear to escape and express the feeling to take on adult responsibilities, and simply psychologically speaking, to take a risk. The true beauty can only be appreciated and admired in its natural state. Birds by nature intended to fly, and ultimately, they should be released from their cages. A bird in a cage may be a symbol of creative spirit, which long to soar and be free of expectations of society, family, or career opportunities. Birds symbolize the authentic voice, vision and passion. It is acceptable to choose the cage for a while as long as it suits the situation, but eventually birds must be released in the wildlife because birds meant to fly and co-exist freely.

> *"The caged bird sings with a fearful trill*
> *of things unknown but longed for still*
> *and his tine is head of the distant hill*
> *for the caged bird sings of freedom."*
> (Maya Angelou "I Know Why the Caged Bird Sings")

However, to understand the 'bird cage' symbol, folks also need to understand the broader context of 'cages' in society. Furthermore, looking at how the bird cage is used in communication, from a psychological perspective, to explore the cage to a container-metaphor that forms people critical thinking, comes out the symbolism of freedom.

The 'bird and cage' as both symbol and metaphor have been used across many transcultural and historical comparisons. There are many references to birds and cages such as *"like a cage full of birds."* (Jeremiah 5:27) Perhaps it symbolized the oppressive situation. The cage would stand for prohibitions and denial of the essentials of life, where is no ways to escape.

The famous phrase written by American poet Maya Angelou states the *"cage bird sings for freedom."* (Angelou, 1983) Angelou contrasts the struggles of a bird attempting to rise above the limitations of adverse surroundings with the flight of a bird that is free. She seeks to create in the reader sentiment toward the plight of the misused, captured creature – a symbol of oppressed African Americans and their experiences.

Bird cage is traditionally associated with the imprisonment – that's why bird cage tattoo with open doors symbolize freedom and liberation. Simultaneously, the empty bird cage flash is a symbol of liberty.

> *"Free to be*
> *Means to be free as a bird.*
> *Freedom and opportunity –*
> *Spread the wings!*
> *Free to sly,*
> *Free to fly!*
> (Tomshinsky, 2017)

When Vasari wrote in *The Lives of the Artists* about the great Leonardo de Vinci that many times he would pass the places, where the birds were sold and kept in cages; he would play the price for letting birds to get out of the cages to fly away into the air, giving them back their lost freedom. This story tells us two things that he had sympathy or perhaps some intellectual gratification for the captive birds in cages, and that he understood the anatomy of birds' wings in fly and never would miss a chance to observe the fascinated to him hollow bones of birds' wings.

It's interesting to reflect on a contemporary installation of the art piece in Sydney, Australia, where bird cages were hung as part of a street-scape art project. The art installation entitled *Empty Birdcages at Angel Place, Sydney*. While the goal was to "source innovative and exciting ideas to temporarily transform [their] city laneways with engaging artworks and inspiring ideas," this comparison appears had an opposite evoking effect – caged life and an absence of freedom, or artlessness in the city. To see the image, please see royalty free image below.

The Chinese Buddhist custom of *fang sheng*, meaning 'release life', proclaimed honors to those who would release birds and animals from cages to freedom. For instant, Tzu-His, the Empress Dowager of China, 1835-1908, each year celebrated her birthday by the release of ten thousand birds. The catchers and merchants would catch the birds and return them back to the markets, to be sold again to the Empress's agents next year. Today, the practice to release birds and animals from cages to freedom continues to be popular among young nature admires in traditional Buddhist communities in Thailand, Cambodia, and Tibet.

"God loved the birds and invented trees. Men loved birds and invented cages." (Jacques Deval) Across many belief-systems and religions, the bird is symbol of the soul. So, a caged bird speaks to an unhealthy inner life or soul. This was the thought that was expressed by Carl Jung in evoking a sense of the caged spirit. Carl Jung said that birds represent thoughts while birds in flight symbolize moving and changing thoughts. Birds are generally associated with freedom and abandon. In old books of dream interpretations, birds are considered lucky omens, except for blackbirds, which are generally symbolize the negativity and darkness. Doves and eagles are generally spiritual symbols. According to Jung, someone's dream depends on its details, but if the birds in one's dream were flying free, it may be symbolic of spiritual, psychological, or physical freedom. (Amar, 2007)

"We have started to confine in prison the animals to which nature had allotted the sky." – stated ancient Roman statesman and scholar Pliny (23-79). He obviously refers to birds and other wild animals' trend to keep them in cages. The *Natural History* by Pliny is a vast encyclopedia full of facts and wisdom of the natural and human worlds.

"The bird, even when caged, remains a symbol of freedom and a stimulus for thinking about the relationship between freedom and human society." (Frederick Jones) One way of thinking about bird cages' presence is that they did speak to the materialism of their owners.

For many people, it is very cruel indeed to catch a free-bird and put in a bird cage. If it was already born in this kind of situation than fine, but also these people prefer to enjoy birds to be outdoors rather than inside a house away from sunshine and nature. Anyone interested in having a bird as a pet really must read *Of Parrots and People* by Mira Tweti. If only every potential bird adopter read this book, demand for caged birds would drop like a rock. For example,

Prince William passionately believes "that we have a duty to prevent critically endangered species from being wiped out."

Most paintings of the Gothic times show them as objects of importance and note within compositions. In a world without radio, it might have been a way of creating a different atmosphere in a house. It's also likely that there were more practical reasons to have birds in cages, outside of aesthetic considerations. Bird cages also were portable storage rooms for hawked owned by peddlers along the streets, as were the birds themselves; and cooks kept birds outside their cages to fatten for the food preparation pleasures.

Also, in the middle of the sixteenth century in England, the expression such as "jailbird" was a common urban jargon term for an incarcerated prisoner. On the streets, people would use related saying, "the bird is flown," meaning that a convicted had escaped.

Across the Atlantic Ocean, American poet Walt Whitman proposed on his poem entitled *My Canary Bird* his sentiments for a song of a caged bird:

"Did we count great, O Soul, to penetrate the themes of mighty books,
Absorbing deep and full from thoughts, plays, speculations?
But now from thee to me, caged bird, to feel the joyous warble,
Filling the air, the lonesome room, the long forenoon,
Is it not just as great, O Soul?"

Today, only six percent of American households keep birds as pets, but in Whitman's time it was different. Before radio and recorded music, songs of birds in cages were among the most popular form of home entertainment. Symbolically, Whitman's canary still remains caged after all these years and displayed in a preserved form under a bell jar in the Boston Museum.

Although as accepted status-symbols, birds and bird cages presence might have been motivation enough, like many cultural trends. For example, *The Birdcage* (1996) comedy features a flamboyant gay couple played by Williams and Lane. "The Birdcage" movie is the hysterically entertaining Americanized version of the French classic *La Cage Aux Folles* (1978). The incredible cast made over-the-top stereotypes funny, instead of just laughable. The movie made the acceptance of the gay culture mainstream. After twenty-year later, the LGBT rights are more talked about and open.

Off all wild life, birds have been always the closest to humankind, and people enjoy to watch their life, observe them seating on a tree or on an electrical poll and appreciate their songs. Birds fly in the sky, the flight ability and birdsongs, make birds exceptionally notable. The mystery surrounded birds sets them apart from other wildlife.

The mystery surrounding of the birds gave born to a wide range of meanings and symbols in literature, more than any other life creatures. For example, the legend of the *Thunderbird* reaches back hundreds of years as part of the mythology of several Native American tribes of the Pacific Northwest and the Great Lakes region. According to the Native American myths, the giant Thunderbird could shoot lightning from its eyes and its wings were so enormous that they created peals of thunder when they flapped. There are many tales of the Thunderbird that are more recent than the Native American legends. A tale comes out of the Arizona Territory desert about two cowboys who encountered the giant flying creature in 1890. As cowboys are accustomed to do, they took careful aim with their rifles at the amazing creature and blasted it from the sky. According to an article in the April 26, 1890 edition of the *Tombstone Epigraph*, the cowboys and their horses dragged the lifeless monster into town, where its wingspan was measured at an incredible 190 feet and its body measured at 92 feet long. It was described as having no feathers, but a smooth skin and wings "composed of a thick and nearly transparent membrane." (Wagner, 2017)

Jerome Clark in his book *Unexplained!* lists many more sightings, including:

- In the early 1940s, writer Robert R. Lyman spotted a Thunderbird sitting on a road near Coudersport, Pennsylvania. It soon took to the sky, spreading its 20-foot wingspan.
- In 1969, the wife of a Clinton County, PA, sheriff saw an enormous bird over Little Pine Creek. She said its wingspan appeared to be about as long as the creek was wide -- about 75 feet!
- In 1970, several people saw the gigantic bird "soaring toward Jersey Shore, PA. It was dark colored, and its wingspread was almost like [that of] an airplane."
- In 1948, several witnesses along the Illinois-Missouri border sighted a condor-like bird about the size of a Piper Club airplane.

In 2001, 2007, and 2013 there were reports of seeing a gigantic enormous bird soaring in Pennsylvania unknown to science, but mentioned in Native American legends and traditions hundred years ago. The most terrifying stories about giant birds is that they occasionally attempt to carry away small animals and even children.

The most amazing are the legends and myth of Phoenix with wise known symbolism of Phoenix rising from ashes back to life. Today, we know that *The Phoenix* was adopted by the early Christianity as a symbol of resurrection. It's also a popular emblem in heraldry:

both Elizabeth I and Mary, the Queen of Scotts, used it as their emblems. Also, it is incorporated in the seal on the flag of the city of Phoenix, Arizona. Originally, it was named Pumpkinville due to the abundance of large pumpkins, growing along the canals, the city was renamed Phoenix upon the suggestion of Lord Darrel Duppa, as it described "a city born from the ruins of a former Hohokam civilization."

In ancient Egyptian mythology, the myth derived the story that Phoenix is a female mythical sacred firebird with beautiful gold and red plumage. Depending on a source, had been said that the firebird lived for 500 or 1461 years. In the legend, Phoenix builds itself a nest of cinnamon twigs that later ignites at the end of its life-cycle. Both nest and bird burn fiercely and are reduced to ashes, from which a new, young and reborn Phoenix arises. The new Phoenix encloses the ashes of the old Phoenix in an egg, made of myrrh, and deposits it in Heliopolis, "the city of the sun" in Greek translation, located in Egypt. The bird was also said had the ability to regenerate when hurt or wounded by an enemy – therefore, being almost immortal and invincible as a symbol of fire and divinity. Originally, the Phoenix was identified by the Egyptians as a stork or heron-like bird called *a bennu*, known from the *Book of the Dead* and other Egyptian texts as one of the sacred symbols of worship at Heliopolis, closely associated with the rising sun and the Egyptian God of Sun *Ra*. One inspiration that has been suggested for the Egyptian Phoenix is flamingo of East Africa. This bird nests on salt flats that are too hot for its eggs or chicks to survive. Therefore, it builds a mound several inches tall and large enough to support its egg, which it lays in that marginally cooler location. The convection currents around these mounds resembles the turbulence of a flame.

The Greeks adapted the word *bennu*. Also took over its further Egyptian meaning of date palm tree, and identified it with their own word Phoenix meaning the color purple-red or crimson *Phoenicia*. They and the Romans subsequently pictured the bird more like a peacock or an eagle. According to the Greeks, the Phoenix lived in Arabia next to a well. At dawn, it bathed in the water of the well, and the Greek God of Sun *Apollo* used to stop the Sun in order to listen to its song. Greek historian Herodotus wrote that priests of ancient Heliopolis described the bird as living for 500 years before building and lighting its own funeral pyre. In Greek mythology, associated with the Sun, a Phoenix obtains new life by arising from the ashes of its predecessor. According to some fascinated sources, the Phoenix dies in a show of flames and combustion, although there are other sources that claim that the legendary bird dies and simply decomposes before being born again.

The most beautiful legend is told about Phoenix as only one Phoenix at a time could live in our world. After a thousand years had passed, the Phoenix had become oppressed by the burden of its age, and the time had come for it to die. To do so, *"the Phoenix had to wing its way into the mortal world, flying westwards across the jungles of Burma, and the torrid plains of India until it reached the scented spice groves of Arabia. Here it collected a bunch of aromatic herbs before setting course for the coast of Phoenicia in Syria. In the topmost branches of a palm tree, the Phoenix constructed a nest out of the herbs and awaited the coming of the new dawn which would herald its death."* (http://www.labyrinthina.com/legend-of-the-phoenix.html)

To this day, the flaming bird inspired countless generations to prolong the tales. In Slavic folklore Phoenix is commonly called the *Firebird*, and it is seen as a majestic flaming bird that glows in bright red-orange color. Legend says, that it's feathers do not case to glow, if one removes them, so just one feather could light a large room, if not covered. (Massie, 1980)

In China and Korea folklore, the *Feng-huang* was associated with the Empress and occupied the high position of ruler of the kingdom of birds. It was frequently paired with a dragon, the symbol of the Emperor, and was held to personalize beauty and mercy. The double

Phoenix represents the male and female principle: *feng* being the male and *huang* the female. For centuries, it has been a favorite motif of artists and artisans throughout East Asia. It most closely resembles an especially colorful bird of paradise with long, flowing tail feathers and a slender neck. *"A mythical bird that never dies. It represents our capacity for vision, for collecting sensory information about our environment and the events unfolding within it. The phoenix, with its great beauty, creates intense excitement and deathless inspiration."* (Lam Kam, Master of Feng Shui. *The Feng Shui Handbook*)

The *Ho-Oo* is the Japanese Phoenix – the Ho being the male bird, and the Oo being the female. Introduced to Japan in the Asuka period at mid-sixth to mid-seventh century A.D., the Hou-Ou greatly resembles in looks the Chinese Phoenix, the Feng-Huang.

Interesting Facts:

Thanks to Japanese hard work in chicken breed, today we have the Phoenix chickens. What is a Phoenix chicken and what is an Onagadori chicken? *Onagadori chickens* are birds with tails that molt only once every three or more years and achieve exceptional tail lengths, from 12 to 27 feet. *Phoenix chickens* are birds that molt each year or every-other-year and tend to have wide, rigid sickle feathers of two to five feet in length and saddle feather of 12 to 18 inches. The Phoenix chicken breed is a result of European attempts to maintain long-tailed fowl working from a small population of imported, Japanese chickens. Also, the Phoenix is an ancient Japanese breed of chicken tracing its heritage back over a thousand years! Symbolically, they are a high-maintenance breed and require special care in order to keep their tail feathers in good shape. Phoenix chickens are recognized by the American Poultry Association as a standard breed in three varieties: Silver (1965); and Golden (1983); Black Breasted Red (approximately 2003). Males weigh 5.5 lbs. and females 4 lbs. It is worth speculating that the name "Phoenix" was given to the resultant chickens to acknowledge the seeming "rise from the ashes" of their soon lost parents.

In ancient Mediterranean and Middle Eastern cultures, as far back as 7,000 years ago, birds were often depicted carrying spirits to the underworld. Jump ahead, a few millennia to 1,550 B.C.E., by which time Ba-birds, depictions of departing souls as human-faced birds, began appearing in Egypt. (Elbein, 2018)

In Greek and Roman mythologies, a harpy (plural harpies) was a half-human and half-bird personification of storm winds, in Homeric poems. *"Bird-bodied, girl-faced things they [Harpies] are; abominable their droppings, their hands are talons, their faces haggard with hunger insatiable,"* – wrote Virgil. (Virgil, n.d.)

Harpies remained vivid in the Middle Ages. In *Canto XIII* of his *Inferno*, Dante Alighieri envisages the tortured wood infested with harpies:

> *"Here the repellent harpies make their nests,*
> *Who drove the Trojans from the Strophades*
> *With dire announcements of the coming woe.*
> *They have broad wings, with razor sharp talons*
> *And a human neck and face."*
> (Dante, n.d.)

William Blake and Gustavo Dorè were inspired by Dante's creepy mystic description in their masterpieces of fine arts. Interesting fact: the harpy eagle is a real bird named after the mythological bird. The word 'harpy' often used in modern English language to describe an angry nasty woman, who is a grasping person, and a gold-digger. It is a derogatory term for a very unpleasant female person. It is often considered offensive to call someone a harpy, in part because it singles out a nasty woman, when a man with similar characteristics might simply be 'loud' or 'opinionated.'

In literature, both non-fiction and fiction, music, and arts, including TV and movies, there are various masterpieces inspired by birds, their mystery and symbols. Please see the list of references to masterpieces where birds taking the center place.

Repurposing Bird Cages in Modern Times

Decorative cages are wonderful pieces for both decoration or to be used as actual bird cages. The practice of making them goes back a couple thousand years, and here are some interesting facts about them.

In modern times, the bird cage can have many different functions accept the main one – to be the bird home. It could be a lovely home decor or it could be given many variations and functions. Some of them are very easy to make. Often people paint the cages in whatever color someone wants or decor them with their favorite flowers or anything else that could be imagined.

Apparently, the idea of decorating with bird cages has been around a lot longer than someone might be thinking. However, today it is almost impossible to pull off at least one historic bird cage's usage, the Marie Antoinette bird cage hairstyle.

> Historic fact: After 1760, women began raising their hair with pads and pomade to a height that towered over their male counterparts. Marie Antoinette took

this trend to the hilt, often undergoing elaborate hairdressing rituals that lifted her hair three feet. Even more astonishing than the height of the hair were the ornaments that decorated the hair, such as birds in cages, Cupids, waterfalls, etc. The most famous of these hairdos was the "Belle Poule," a model of a French frigate or naval vessel.

Yet, a true story – professor meets a student at the student Halloween party in the nineties: a reflection to the history trend in a blue bird cage head attire to the male's all-blue costume.

Predominantly, the bird cages influenced entertaining industry, fashion attire, and, of course, the interior design of both interiors and exteriors. The 'birdcage' veil business brings a new trend with vintage look to fashion wedding attire. Reese Witherspoon wore a bird cage veil in the movie *Sweet Home Alabama* (2002), which people approved, copied, and fell in love with. There are various elegant bird cage headgear pieces for wedding veils, hats, and fascinators. For a wedding, every detail matters, and the feathers and tulle fabric create a special distinct 'bird cage effect.'

The nature-lovers would happy to know that there are plentiful amount of bird and cage fabrics; sometimes, the image of the textile print various to black cat mesmerized by the bird in cage. The same way as women are wrapping their bodies in fabrics with whimsical prints of butterflies and birds, cherries and chairs, flowers and animals, and many more beloved objects, beautiful fabric with bird cages affectionate children's pajamas, grandmother's aprons, women's summer-statement dresses and skirts. The industry of T-shirts design also contributed to both the bird-cage image and graphic typography of the words 'birdcage' or 'bird cage.'

More recently, the spring correspondence appeared with lovely birds and bird cages address labels.

Jewelry fashion accessories embrace the birds and bird cages motif in brooches, earrings, and pendants. The vintage women's gold-tone French bird cage and bird earrings would add style and chic to any main outfit. The authentic vintage and most wanted bird cages earrings have been worn by many celebrities including Jessica Simpson, Kim Kardashian, Kelly Osbourne, and Beyoncé. All accents are done in gold-metal with a bird cage design throughout. The top button leads to crisscross bars with a dangling 'CC' signature logo trapped inside. Betsy Johnson's mouse-ballerina and the birdcage or Lonna & Lilly's gold-tone basket bird cage with gemstone drop earrings will spice up any spring and summer attire. The famous French fashion designer, Karl Lagerfeld, used the bird cage to pay tribute to Chanel. The idea came from a little gold bird cage that sat upon the Holy Bible in Coco Chanel's apartment in Paris.

The http://www.thefashionbirdcage.com/ website emphasizes on dressing or undressing the body with cloth and fashion accessories. Young women would adore the sexy high-heel women's platform so-called strappy 'bird cage' shoes. The weird fashion published by www.funfashion.org. The weird fashion moment may include 3-dimenssial bird cages with a bird or without it in front of the dress' attachment. Sometimes, there are birds or bird-eggs-in-a-nest as a headgear. As odder the design, the more attention from weird fashion application. Fashion designers keep themselves busy exposing creativity on runways' fashion lines. Elegant purses and handbages use bird cages as ornamenation and to ador the main outfit with 'weird' fashion accessory, which guards the individual belongings safe the same as a bird-in-the-cage. For instant, Dua Lipa can wear anything to make a moment. For the *Alita: Battle Angel* premiere, Dua opted for a black and white dress from Armani Prive, shaped as a strapless bodysuit and cage-structured skirt, all in one piece. Of course, the birdcage-like gown represented the chicest red carpet's fashion moments.

Here is a story that is reflecting on bird cage balconies in architectural building of Victorian style. During the height of the silver boom, from 1881 to 1889, the *Bird Cage Theatre* was opened in Tombstone, Arizona. It was a combination of a saloon, gambling parlor, and brothel under the roof of the Victorian architectural style building. Of course, there was a different use of the so-called bird cages or birdcages. In a way, it was how wild American West influenced the Victorian style entertaining.

> Historic facts: The *Bird Cage Theatre* was owned by Lottie and William "Billy" Hutchinson. Hutchison, a variety performer, originally intended to present to respectable families shows like the one he had seen in San Francisco and that were packed by large crowds. After the Theatre opened, Hutchinson hosted the Ladies Nights for the respectable women of Tombstone, who could attend performances for free. But the economics of Tombstone did not support their aspirations. They soon canceled the Ladies Nights and began offering not so noble entertainment that appealed to the rough-minded crowd. It gained a reputation as one of the wickedest theaters between New Orleans and San Francisco. There were fourteen cages or boxes on two balconies. These boxes, also known as cribs, featured drapes that patrons could use while entertained by show girls.

The building was not opened again until it was purchased in 1934, and the new owners were delighted to find out that almost nothing had been disturbed in all those years. It has been a tourist attraction ever since, and is open to the public year-round.

In 21st century, many people use their creativity to decorate their apartments with the bird cages, by repurposing them and making the bamboo bird cage into a wind chime, painted bird cages into succulent displays, or the small-size bird cages in matching lanterns. Some enthusiastic gardeners successfully use the bird cages in outdoors gardening with plants and flowers; sometimes, with artificial birds.

People often ask when the trend of decorating with bird cages started? Perhaps when one bird pet was left free in the wild nature in the common habitat. When does a bird cage look the most beautiful and appealing? Maybe when it is not actually confining any bird inside it! Of course, that leaves one free, happy bird and an empty bird cage that got the need to be put to good use. Seriously, there is something special about adding a bird cage into the decor mix of a room – it has a special informal bohemian vibe, the Victorian feel, kind of a special decorative touch.

The ideas to use bird s for décor are endless. The bird cages bring on nostalgic rustic atmosphere to any space. Kitchens, bed and bath barrowed the bird cage motif for shower curtains and cotton kitchen towels, and chic aprons to keep on with updated trends in home décor. There are stands and flat racks that are in the shape of a bird cage. The flat ones are used to display books or hang up photographs, or to hang and organize jewelry in residentials interiors. People reusing bird cages for storage solutions to bring both elegance and rustic chic in the home décor. It is a creative storage solution for mail and cards' holdings and display. Some people store Christmas ornaments in the vintage bird cages to make unique stylish Christmas decoration statement.

Bird cages help to create unique centerpiece arrangements for any celebration. Bird cage can be used as an elegant accessory at the table centerpiece for a country wedding, mid-summer party, and special events. The guest name-tags cards use elegant silver bird cages for upscale occasions. Bird cages are widely used for lighting to bring up the shabby chic pendant light fixtures. People use both – house the candles in them and stuff the bird cages with strand of string-lights to create the special image of the industrial lighting design. A little bird cage is an interesting alternative to a candle lantern. The gorgeous vintage bird cage would be a great décor piece by itself – next to a potted plant or a vintage mirror frame. The hardcover antique books inside a large bird cage would bring the country rustic chic that would any librarian envy.

The great outdoors is a great inspiration for repurposing bird cages to use them as a hanging planter or bohemian decor pieces. The bird cages would highlight any porch decoration. Decorative bird cages for sale can cost thousands. Some are gilded in gold or covered in hand-carved designs of wood, silver, or gold and other precious metals. These cages are also found as antiques items of the Victorian era. To find decorative bird cages today could be difficult. Antique stores or online vendors are the best sources. The online antique dealers are very though, and it is impossible to verify what the item is worth with only few photos. Many people collect antique bird cages and bird cage's objects of Victorian era such as automation singing bird music boxes such as Jaquez Droz's double-duty singing bird and clock made in Germany, or gilt bronze singing bird cage attributed to Charles Abraham Brunguier made in Geneva, c.1840. They are very rare and infrequent.

Enamel musical box in the form of a bird cage plays
Papageno's song from the *Magic flute* by W. A. Mozart.

There is no need to repurpose these little work of art.

Thanks to bird cages' unique shape, bird cages bring plenty of visual
and textural contrast to any space that they adorn with. They also
give an interesting little style spin for both a modern city loft and a
country vintage line.

No argument that bird cages have gone through a decor transformation.
They are no longer are only for holding birds, but instead encase

flowers, chocolates, and wedding favors. Bird cages decorations are desired by wedding designers who have devised charming ways to use these inexpensive items as centerpieces. Obviously, they are in the category of 'something old' or vintage.

There are various decorative do-it-yourself (DIY) projects that may satisfy any taste and style.

In some cultures, a bird cage represents captivity or entrapment. Most cultures, see decorative bird cages as wonderful works of art. Antique decorative bird cages have sold for thousands, and not just depending on material. Some have interesting histories or are so elaborately designed that buyers cannot turn them down. Because there are many different cultural traditions, from the Far East to the West, as birds had been kept as pets for thousands of years, it is impossible to tell who first began making these bird cages as works-of-art.

One thing is for sure, the bird cages once were solely owned by royalty and aristocrats; but today, everybody might have a chance to own one.

The baker industry made some adaptations as well. The bird cage cake-toppers are guarding the cakes from damage. Of course, the artist cake-makers' imitations to bake up a look-a-like cake in full size of a birdcage with marzipan bird- figurines will win any contest or baking competition.

The antique stores all over the country proudly display the porcelain statues of ladies with bird cages and bird-catchers with bird cages outdoors, whimsical teapots in bird cages style to serve amazing tea parties, Art DECO vases and jars; and even, the HIGGINS fused art glass birds on gilded cages of ashtrays. These ashtrays probably are coming out from Los Vegas casinos, circa the casino's golden age, circa late fifties.

For the mass production, there are countless wall art and home décor art deals with the bird cages as a focal point. The same goes for the fine arts with bird cages at national and world art studios and museums.

A good sample of fine arts would be the Georg Frederich Kersting's painting entitled *Two Children with Parrot Cage*, completed c.1835. Obviously, the bird cage with a parrot pet bird subject is taking the main attractiveness next to the two children fascinated by the exotic bird. Their body language tells the story of the parrot's admiration. And of course, they are learning their lesson on wildlife. Georg Friedrich Kersting was a German painter, best known for his Biedermeier-style interior paintings.

The Birdcage, 1910. Oil on canvas
Frederick Carl Frieseke (1874-1939),
American Impressionist painter.

This painting by Frieseke had been made in the beginning of the 20th century. Frederick Carl Frieseke, who was born in Owosso, Michigan, represents American Impressionist movement. He graduated from Art Institute of Chicago and *Academie Julian* in Paris. He spent most of his life as an expatriate in France. Beside *The Birdcage, Open Window* also known as (*The Birdcage*), and *Yellow and Blue* are museum quality premium archival prints reproductions that will satisfy the taste of any bird and cage art lovers.

For modern contemporary art, bird and cage admirers may use the Birdcage Fine Art Studio, which started out as a working studio in Eureka Springs, in Arkansas, led by artist R. P. Irvin. Several local artists came on board, and there was a need for a space to show and sell their art. Today, it is a unique collection of paintings, ceramics, jewelry, fabric arts, sculpture and wood-work.

Perhaps, there is a nostalgia for good-quality bird cages motivated by collecting antiques, or simply, have a longing for the birds' songs indoors. Then comes the question: why so much noise about birds and cages? I think in the digital age when search, access, and results are electronically fast, birds and cages remind us about nature, flora and fauna on our beautiful planet, the Earth. No matter where we live, the songs of birds brighten up our days. This is the nature's orchestra at its best! The early morning chirps of a robin or chickadee delight us, and the sound of a honking flock of migrating geese inspire us.

Guide to the Masterpieces in Literature, TV, and Movies, Where Birds are Taking the Central Part, Literary or Symbolic

Ackerman, Jennifer. (2017) *The Genius of Birds.*
Alderman, David. (2018) *The Complete Illustrated Encyclopedia of Birds of the World: A Detailed Visual Reference Guide.*

Alderson, David. (2014) *The Ultimate Encyclopedia of Caged and Aviary Birds: Practical Family Reference Guide to Keeping Pet Birds, with Expert Advice on Buying, Understanding, Breeding and Exhibiting Birds.*

Amstutz, Lisa. (2016) *Blue Jays. – (Backyard Birds.)*

Anders, Charlie Jane. (2017) *All the Birds in the Sky.*

Anderson, Hans Christian. (1999) *The Ugly Duckling.*

Angelou, Maya. (2009) *I know Why the Caged Bird Sings.*

Aristophanes. (2015) The *Birds.*

Aslet, Clive. (2014) *The Birdcage's Manuel.*

Athan, Mattie Sue. (2005) *Parrots: Complete Pet Owner.*

Augelini, Jude. (2017) *The Hummingbird: Essays.*

Banks, Edwin. (2018) *Little Ethan and His Feathered Friend.*

Bannick, Paul. (2016) *Owls: A Year in the Lives of North American Owls.*

Barcott, Bruce. (2009) *The Last Flight of Scarlet Macaw: One Women's Flight to Save the World's Most Beautiful Bird.*

Beadle, David and James D. Rising. (2001*) Sparrows of United States and Canada: The Photographic Guide.*

Beechman, Andrew D. (2007) *Pigeons: A Fascinating Saga of the World's Most Revered and Reviled Bird.*

Berman, Ruth and Richard Hewett. (1996) *Peacocks. – (Early Bird Nature Book).*

Blakemore, Victoria. (2017) *Flamingos.*

Blue Bird: DVD. – Shirly Temple (Actress)

Blue, Debbie. (2013) *Consider the Birds: A Provocative Guide to Birds of the Bible.*

Bodden, Valerie. (2018) *Peacocks. – (Amazing Animals)*

Bree, Marlin. (2011) *Amazing Gulls: Acrobats of the Sky and Sea.*

Brown, Lolly. (2016) *Canary as Pets: Canary Breeding, Diet, Cages, Singing, Where to Buy, Cost, Health, Lifespan, Types, and More Covered! The Ultimate Canary Care Guide.*

Brown, Lolly. (2016) *Cockatoos: Cockatoo Facts & Information, Where to Buy, Health, Diet, Lifespan, Types, Breeding, Fun Facts and More! Complete Cockatoo Pet Guide.*

Bryant, Megan E. (2006) *Happy Feet: The Movie Storybook.*

Byrne, Kevin Michael. (2013) *Duck Dynasty: Family Faith and Family Fun.*

Canning, Victor. (1979) *Birdcage.*

Carr, Aaron. (2015) *Dodo. – (Extinct Animal0.*

Cavanaugh, Nancy A. (2017) *Emu: A Curious Bird.*

Chekhov, Anton. (1896) *The Seagull*

Cheeves, Ann. (2017) The Crow: A Vera Stenhope Mystery.

Cheeves, Ann. (20017) *The Seagull: A Vera Stenhope Mystery.*

Churchill, Abby. (1911) *Birds in Literature.*

Collard III, Sneed B. and Robin Brickman (2002) *Beaks!*

Copeland, Misty and Cristopher Myers. (2014) *Firebird.*

D'Arcy, Paula. (2002) *Gift of Red Cardinal: The Story of Divine Encounter.*

Dave, Frederic and David Bellos. (2016) *Bird in a Cage.*

Davies, Nick. (2015) *Cuckoo: Cheating by Nature.*

De Bernieres, Louise. (2005) *Birds Without Wings.*

Dickenson, Rachel. (2009) *Falconer at the Edge: A Man, His Bird, and the Vanishing of the American West.*

Drabble, Margaret. (2013) *A Summer Bird-Cage: A Novel.*

Duck Dynasty Season 11: The Final Season. (2017). – DVD.

Dunmore, Helen. (2017) *The Birdcage Walk.*

Dunn, Mary R. (2015) *Turkey Vultures: Birds of Prey.*

Earley, Chris. (2003) *Sparrow and Finches of the Great Lakes Region and Eastern North America.*

Elliot, Zetta and Sandra Stickland. (2017) *Bird.*

Ellis, Eliana M. (2011) *Write about an Empty Birdcage.*

Elphick, Jonathan (2016) *A Complete Guide to Biology and Behavior.*

Erdrich, Louse. (2009) *The Plaque of Doves.*

Fadel, Youssef and Jonathan Smolin. (2017) *A Rare Blue Bird Flies with Me:* Novel.

Fallon, Katie. (2018) *Vulture: Private Life of Unloved Bird.*

Fleischman, Paul and Ken Nutt. (1989) *I Am Phoenix: Poems of Two Voices.*

Fogden, Michael and Marianne Taylor. (2014) *Hummingbirds: A Life-size Guide to Every Species.*

Forshaw, Joseph M. and Frank Knight. (2010) *Parrots of the World.*

Gibbs, Maddie. (2011) *Flamingos. – (Safari Animals).*

Gorman, Mary. (2005) *Love Birds: Complete Pet Owner's Manuel.*

Guertin, Anne Marie and Helena Perez Garcia. (2018) *How the Finch Got His Color.*

Guravish, Dan and Joseph E. Brown. (1983) *The Return of the Brown Pelican.*

Gustafson, Scott. (2016) *The Favorite Nursery Rhymes from Mother Goose.*

Happy Feet: DVD.

Hall, Mark, Mark Lee Rollins, and Loren Coleman. (2004) *Thunderbirds: America's Living Legends of Giant Birds.*

Hitchcock, Alfred. 91963) *The Birds:* DVD.

Hodgkiss, Phil. (2014) *Gulls!*

Hoose, Phillip. (2016) *The Race to Save the Lord God Bird.*

Hughes, Janes M. (2008) *Cranes: A Natural History of Birds in Crises*

Hurst, Camila and Joana Mendes. (2017) *A Little Bird in a Cage.*

Hyland, Angus. (2016) *A Book of Birds: Birds in Art.*

Jaggard, Victoria. (2018) *The Dinosaurs That Didn't Die. – National Geographic,* May, pp. 78-97.

Kelly, Joseph. (2017) *The Seagull Book of Poems.*

Kessler, Brad and Robert Van Nutt. (2013) *The Firebird:* The Classic Russian Fairy Tale.

Kiernan, Stephen P. (2016) *The Hummingbird: Novel.*

Kousky, Vern. (2017) *The Blue Songbird.*

Kramer, Gary. (2018) *Game Birds: A Celebration of North American Upland Birds.*

LaFayette, M.Y. (2018) *Birdcage.*

Laurence, Margaret. (1993) *A Bird in the House:* Stories.

Layman, John and Mike Marts. (2018) *Eleonor and the Egret.*

Lee, Harper. (2017) *To Kill the Mockingbird.*

Linde, Barbara M. (2012) *The Bizarre Life Cycle of Cuckoo.*

Link, Kimberley (2014) *The Ultimate Pet Duck Guidebook: All the Things You Need to Know Before Bringing Home Your Feathered Friend.*

Linz, Geords M. and Michael L. Avery. (2017) *Ecology and Management of Blackbirds [Icteridae] in North America.*

Loying, Denton. (2014) *Crimes Against Birds: Poems.*

Lutwack, Leonard. (1994) *Birds in Literature.*

Martin, Steve. (2011) *Rare Bird Alert Tablature Book.*

Massie, Suzanne. (1980) *Land of the Firebird: The Beauty of Old Russia.*

Materlinck, Maurice and Alexander Teixeira De Matos. (2018) *The Blue Bird:* A Fairy Play in Six Acts.

May, Elaine and Mike Nicholas. (2017) *The Birdcage: A Shooting Script.*

Mayo, Margaret and Peter Bailey. (2003) *The Incredible Thunderbird. – (Magical Tales from Around the World S.)*

McCarthy, Michael. (2016) *Say Goodbye to the Cuckoo: Migratory Birds and the Impending Ecological Catastrophe.*

McCloskey, Robert. (2016) *Make Way for Ducklings.*

McMeekin, Ross. (2018) *The Hummingbirds: A Novel.*

MacIver, Roderick. (2011) *The Heron Dance Book of Love and Gratitude.*

Mikkola, Heimo. (2013) *Owls of the World: A Photographic Guide to 1600 Birds and Their Habitats, Shown in More Than 1800 Pictures.*

Mikulica, Oldrich and Tomas Grim. (2017) *The Cuckoo: The Uninvited Guest.*

Mounstaki, Nikky. (2005) *Parrots for Dummies.*

Murzluff, John, and Tony Angell. (2013) *Gifts of the Crow: How Perception, Emotion, and Thought Allow Smart Birds to Behave Like Humans.*

Niemann, Derek. (2013) *Bird in a Cage.*

Nigg, Joseph. (2016) *The Phoenix: An Unnatural Biography of Mythical Beast.*

Norsk, Caroline. (2016) *Pigeons: Amazing Photos & Fun Facts Book About Pigeons for Kids.*

O'Brian, Stacey. (2009) *Wesley the Owl: The Remarkable Love Story of an Owl and His Girl.*

O'Connor, Mike (2007) *Why Don't Woodpeckers Get Headaches? And Other Bird Questions You Know You Want to Ask.*

O'Connor, Rebecca. (2008) *Fitches. – (Animal planet & Pet Care Library)*

Okri, Ben. (1995) *Birds of Haven.*

Oliver, Mary. (2009) *Red Bird: Poems.*

Oregon Fish and Game Commission and Jackson Chambers. (2018) *Pheasant Farming.*

Ormondroyd, Edward and Joan Rasor. (2012) *David and the Phoenix.*

Ow, Anya. (2016) *The Firebird Tale.*

Peterson, Roger Tory. (2005) *Audubon's Birds of America.*

Polette, Nancy. (1990) *Birds in Literature: A Whole Language Activity Book.*

Poe, Edgar Allan. (2017) *Raven.*

Read, Tracy. (2011) *Exploring the World of Owls.*

Rockwell, Anne and Megan Halsey. (2003) *Two Blue Jays.*

Rodendale, Roger. (2016) *Emu: Emus as Pets: Emus Keeping, Care, Housing, Interaction, Diet and Health.*

Roher, Rebecca. (2016) *Bird in a Cage.*

Rose, Caroline Starr. (2016) *Blue Bird.*

Rucker, Gabriel and Meredith Erickson. (2013) *Le Pigeon: Cooking at the Dirty Bird.*

Rutledge, Archibard. (2016) *The Egret's Plums.*

Sartori, Breanne. (2014) *Peacocks: Amazing Pictures and Facts About Peacocks.*

Savage, Candace. (2015) *Crows: Encounters with the Wise Guys of the Avian World.*

Savage, Katie and Emily Marie Henebrey. (2017) *Not Especially Special.*

Schraff, Anne E. (2005) *Bird in a Cage.*

Sesame Street. (1990) *Big Bird is Yellow: A Sesame Street Book of Color.*

Shalev, Meir. (2009) *Pigeon and a Boy: Novel.*

Simmons, Rulon and Bates Littlehales. (2006) *National Geographic Photographing Birds.*

Skye, Brielle. (2014). *Solitude of a Birdcage.*

Silverman, Buffy. (2016) *Can You Tell an Ostrich from an Emu? – (Lighting Bolt Books.)*

Soucek, Gayle A. (2006) *Doves: Pet Complete Owner's Manuel.*

Spirin, Gennady and Tatiana Popova. (2002) *The Tale of Firebird.*

Staake, Bob. (2013) *Bluebird.*

Stravinsky, Igor. (2002) *Firebird:* DVD. – Royal Danish Ballet.

Strattin, Lisa. (2016) *Facts About the Snowy Egret.*

Strycker, Noah and Joel Sartore. (2018) *Birds of the Photo Ark.*

Strunk, Stephen. (2016*) Peterson Reference Guide to Woodpeckers of North America.*

Suskind, Patrick. (1989) *Pigeon.*

Tafuri, Nancy. (1996*) Have You See My Duckling?*

Taylor, Marianne. (2016) *Owls: A Guide to Every Species in the World.*

Tchaikovsky, Piotr. (2007) *Swan Lake:* DVD.

Tekeila, Stan. (2016) *Cranes, Herons & Egrets: The Elegance of Our Tallest Birds.* – (Wildlife Appreciation.)

Tekeila, Stan. (2016) *Woodpeckers. – (Backyard Bird Feeding Guides).*

The Angry Birds. (2016): DVD.

The Story of Swan Lake (N. d.): Audio CD. – London Philharmonic Orchestra.

The Tale of Ivan Tsarevich, The Firebird, and the Gray Wolf: Russian Tale.

Tkekhlebov, Alexey Vasilyevich. (2014) *Legends of the Phoenix: Tales of Forgotten Past.*

Tomshinsky, Ida. (2007) *Fascinated by Gulls: Poems.*

Unwin, Mike, David Tipling and Tony Angell. (2017) *The Enigma of the Owl: An Illustrated Natural History.*

Vail, Grace. (2016*) A Bird Watcher's Guide to Sparrows. – (Backyard Bird Watchers).*

Vermont Department of Fish and Game and Jackson Chambers. (2018) Instructions for the Raising of Pheasants.

Wingate, Marty. (2018) *Farewell, My Cuckoo: A Bird of Feather Mystery.*
Yolen, Jane. (2014) *Fine Feathered Friends:* Poems for Young People.
Zuckerman, Andrew. (2009) *Birds.*

REFERENCES

Aesop's Fables: A New Translation by Laura Gibbs. (2002) – Oxford University Press (World's Classics): Oxford.

Angelou, Maya. (1983) *Cage Bird:* [Poem from *Shaker*]: *Why Don't You Sing? – The Complete Collected Poems of Maya Angelou* (Random House Inc., 1994).

Armistead, George L. & Brian L. Sullivan. (2015) *Better Birding: Tips, Tools, and Concepts for the Field.* – Princeton. – 360 pages.

Attenborough, David. (1998) *The Life of Birds.* – Princeton. – 320 pages.

Axelson, Gustave. (2016) *In Colombia, Shade-Grown Coffee Sustaining Songbirds and People Alike.* – Retrieved on August 24, 2018 at http://allaboutbirds.org.

Bhattacharjee, Yudhijit. (2018) *Epic Journeys. – National Geographic*, 2018, p. 30-59.

Bee, Dianne. (1992) *Bird Cages to Crochet: Five Designs.* – Leisure Arts Leaflet. – 6 pages.

Bechstein, J. M. (2012) *The Natural History of Cage Birds, Their Management, Habits, Food, Diseases, Treatment, Breeding, and the Methods of Catching Them.* – A Public Domain Book. – 675 pages.

Bird Cages: Royalty Free Stock Photo. – Retrieved on February 21, 2017 at http://cdn.pixabay.com/birdcages

Birkhead, Tim. (2014) *Ten Thousand Birds: Ornithology since Darwin.* – Princeton. – 544 pages.

Brown, Lolly. (2016) *Canary as Pets: Canary Breeding, Diet, Cages, Singing, Where to Buy, Cost, Health, Lifespan, Types, and More Covered!* – NRB Publishing. – 108 pages.

Bruns, Roger A. (2000) *Desert Honkytonk: The Story of Tombstone's Bird Cage Theatre.* – Fulcrum Publishing. – 208 pages.

Carini, Simona. (2018) *Conversation.* – *AJN*, Vol. 118, No. 3, p.33.

Corbin, Shawndrea. (2014) *Vintage Birdcages.* – *Phoenix Home & Garden*, 2014, p. 40. https://www.petcha .com/history-of-pet-bird-cages

Dennis, Jerry. (2014) *A History of Captive Birds.* – *University of Michigan Library*: Michigan Publishing, Summer 2014, Vol. 53, Issue 3. – Retrieved on June 29, 2018 from http://handle. net/2017/spo.act2080.0053.301

Elbein, Asher. (2018) *Sirens of Greek Myth Were Bird-Women, Not Mermaids.* – Retrieved on April 6, 2018 from http://www.audubon. org/news/sirens-greek-myth-were-bird-women-not-mermaids

Emery, Nathan. (2016) *Bird Brain: An Exploration of Avian Intelligence.* – Princeton. – 192 pages.

Forshaw, Joseph Michael. (2010) *Parrots of the World.* – Princeton. – 336 pages.

Goldberg, Susan. (2018) *'If You Take Care of the Birds, You Take Care of Most of the Big Problems in the World.'* – National Geographic, Vol. 233, No. 1, p. 4.

Harris, Steve. (2010) *Feral Pigeon: Flying Rat or Urban Hero?* – Retrieved from March 28, 2017 at http://www.discoverwildlife.com/british -wildlife/feral-pigeon-flying-rat-or-urban-hero

Hill, Karen. (2008) *When Did Pigeons Carry the Mail?* – Retrieved from April 3, 2017 at http://superbeefy.com

Imes, Rick. (1991) *North American Bird Identifier.* – Mallard Press: New York. – 80 pages.

Jacob, Laura. (2010) *Bird Catcher.* – Picador. – 304 pages.

Kale, Herbert W. (1990) *Florida's Birds.* – Sarasota: Pineapple Press. – 288 pages.

Kane, Kathryn. (2014) *Popinjay Palaces: Bird Cages in the Regency.* – Retrieved from February 27, 2017 at http://regencyredingone. wordpress.com

Kilmer, Nicholas, David Sellin & Barbara H. Weinberg. (2001) *Frederick Carl Frieseke: An Evolution of an American Impressionist.* – Princeton University Press. – 216 pages.

Leahy, Christopher W. (2006) *Birdwatcher's Companion to North American Birdlife.* – Princeton. – 1072 pages.

Lovitch, Derek. (2012) *How to Be a Better Birder.* – Princeton. – 208 pages.

McBride, Abby. (2012) *Wildlife-Trafficking – Bust Highlight Problems in Caged Bird Trade.* – Retrieved on January 6, 2018 from http:// www.allaboutbirds.org

Morris, Megan. (2014) *Decorating with Bird Cages:* [eBook] – Rudecolor.com. – 4621 KB

Mozart, Wolfgang and Silver Tonalities. (2016) *Papageno, The Bird Catcher's Song: The Magic Flute Beginner Tots Piano Sheet Music.* – Silver Tonalities. – 5 pages.

Norris, Anna. (2014) *15 Birds with Snazzier Hairdos That You.* – Retrieved on 5 January 5, 2018 from http://www.mnn. com/nov/4/2014

Nothingam, Sherry. (2014) *Decorating with Birdcages: 30 Creative Ideas.* – Retrieved from February 22, 2017 at http://decoist.com

Pangman, Judy. (2006) *Chicken Coops: 45 Building Ideas for Housing Your Flock.* – Storey Publishing. – 176 pages.

Ponsot, Marie. (1999) *The Bird Catcher: Poems.* – Knopf. – 104 pages.

Randall Jr., Richard H. (1953) *A Gothic Bird Cage.* – Jstor: The Metropolitan Museum of Art, p.286-292. – Retrieved from www.jstor.org

Roberts, Sonia. (1973) *Bird-Keeping and Birdcages: A History/1st Edition.* -Drake Publishers. – 138 pages.

Serjeantson, Dale. (2009) *Birds.* – Cambridge University Press: Cambridge. – 512 pages.

Silvana Amar, Silvana. (2007) *Bedside Dream Dictionary.* – Skyhorse Publishing, Inc.

Spillman, Benjamin. (2018) *"Mass Killing" of Raptors Leads to Charges Against California Man.* – Retrieved on March 15, 2018 at <u>https://www.msn.com/en-us/news/crime/mass-killing'-of-raptors-leads-to-charges-against-California-man/ar-BBKe9zt?ocid=spartandhp.</u>

The Andrew B. Hendryx Company Knew Why Caged Birds Sing. (2013) - Retrieved from February 20, 2017 at <u>http://www.hagley.org/librarynews/andrew-b-hendryx-company-knew-why-caged-birds-sing</u>

The History of Bird Cages. (2014) – Retrieved on February 20, 2017 at <u>http://blog.michaels.com/blog/the-history-of-bird-cages</u>

Thompson, Bill. (1997) *Bird Watching for Dummies: Miniature Editions.* – Running Press. – 128 pages.

Tilford, Tony. (2001) *The Cage & Aviary Bird Handbook.* – New Holland. – 144 pages.

Verhoef, Esther. (2003) *Complete Encyclopedia of Cage and Aviary Birds.* – Rebo Books. – 350 pages.

Walcott, Derek. (2011) *White Egrets.*

World Through the Lens. (2012) – Retrieved on March 11, 2017 at <u>http://worldthoughthelens/family-history/old-occupations.php</u>

Zuckerman, Catherine. (2018) *Solving Crimes Against Birds.* – *National Geographic*, Vol. 233, No. 1, p. 15.

<u>http://reference.com/pets-animals/difference-between-dove-pigeon-e8655e5541dc90a3</u>

<u>www.HandmadeBirdcages.com</u>